THE
CONDUCT OF
MEETINGS

Norton Rose
Blackfriars House
London EC4V 6DH

THE CONDUCT OF MEETINGS

23rd edition

Edited by

Mandy Burton LLB
Formerly Lecturer in Law, University of Leicester

Fiona Patfield BA, LLB, LLM
Senior Research Fellow in Company and Commercial Law,
Institute of Advanced Legal Studies, University of London;
Lecturer in Law, University of Leicester

Norton Rose
Blackfriars House
London EC4V 6DH

jORDANS

1994

Published by
Jordan Publishing Limited
21 St Thomas Street
Bristol BS1 6JS

British Library Cataloguing-in-Publication Data
A catalogue record for this book is available from the British Library.

ISBN 0 85308 098 4

Typeset by Create Publishing Services Limited
Printed in Great Britain by Henry Ling Limited, The Dorset Press, Dorchester

PREFACE

Since the last edition of this book, there have been substantial changes in the relevant law and this new edition has been extensively updated to incorporate these changes.

Legislative developments of particular note are the Public Order Act 1986, the Companies Act 1985, the Insolvency Act 1986 and the Local Government (Access to Information) Act 1985. The Public Order Act 1986 is covered in Part II by Mandy Burton, who also rewrote the whole of Part IV to reflect the provisions of the Local Government (Access to Information) Act 1985. Part III, edited by Fiona Patfield, deals with the relevant aspects of the Companies Act 1985 and the Insolvency Act 1986. In addition, the general principles in Part I have been reviewed jointly by the authors.

Special thanks are due to Mrs Jay Parkin of the Institute of Advanced Legal Studies for her invaluable secretarial assistance during the revision of the book.

The law is stated as at 1 May 1994.

FIONA PATFIELD
MANDY BURTON
London
May 1994

CONTENTS

TABLE OF CASES

TABLE OF STATUTES

TABLE OF STATUTORY INSTRUMENTS

PART I

MEETINGS: GENERAL PRINCIPLES

CHAPTER 1

MEETINGS

Meetings dealt with in this book are of two main types:

(1) 'public meetings', being meetings convened by individuals or bodies and to which there is an open invitation extended to any member of the public;
(2) meetings of bodies of which the members are limited.

Meetings of both categories are governed to some extent by the general law. In addition, meetings of the second category are normally governed by by-laws or regulations relating to the convening and conduct of the meetings and ancillary matters. These by-laws or regulations may be statutory (eg for meetings of local authorities) or they may exist by agreement between the members of the corporation or association concerned (such, for example, are the relevant articles of association of a company incorporated under the Companies Acts). For public meetings, on the other hand, there will not be any such by-laws or regulations. To a limited extent there may be regulations imposed by government or local authorities which impose restrictions or obligations, but that is all.

This book is concerned principally with meetings which fall into the second category. The commonest type of such bodies is the company incorporated under the Companies Acts; in addition, there are companies incorporated under particular Acts, companies incorporated by charter, local authorities, clubs, trade associations, trade unions, unit trusts, industrial and provident societies, friendly societies, building societies, sporting associations, political associations, ad hoc committees set up for particular purposes, local amenity committees and numerous other bodies.

The principles relating to meetings apply to meetings of all such bodies. Actual detailed provisions will vary in every case, as needs vary: for example, the needs of the Amateur Athletic Association are different from the needs of a local cricket club, or a local anti-litter society, and these in turn are different from those of a large public company with several thousand shareholders. There are differences between meetings of the governing body of an association (eg the directors of a company or the executive committee of a political association) and meetings of the members, but the principles are the same for all such meetings.

Part I deals with meetings in general and, where convenient, mentions particular requirements for certain types of bodies. Public meetings are discussed in Part II; meetings of companies incorporated under the Companies Act 1985 are discussed in Part III; and meetings of local authorities are discussed in Part IV. These separate parts must all be read in the light of, and subject to, the general principles in Part I.

The matters to be considered in relation to meetings can conveniently be broken up into separate headings:

(1) Who may attend, and how are meetings convened?
(2) What constitutes a valid meeting and what business may be dealt with?
(3) How is the meeting conducted?
(4) How are decisions recorded?

The following chapters of Part I answer these questions in general terms. These general terms apply to all bodies except insofar as statutes or their own regulations make modifications.

CHAPTER 2

THE CONVENING OF MEETINGS

Introduction

Before a meeting can be duly constituted, it must have been duly convened. The body concerned will usually have regulations providing for this. These will state who may call meetings, who is to be entitled to receive notice, how notice is to be given and the information to be contained in the notice.

In the case of a company incorporated under the Companies Acts, most of the provisions as to meetings are to be found in the company's articles of association or in the Act. These are dealt with in Part III. Similarly, in the case of local authorities there are various rules contained in statutes which govern the holding of meetings, and these are dealt with in Part IV. Other bodies may be subject to their own rules as to meetings.

There is, however, a number of general principles applicable to most meetings. It should be borne in mind that the principles stated in this Part will apply only where the relevant rules governing the meeting in question do not otherwise provide. The application of these principles is considered further in Chapter 14.

Notices and agenda

So that a meeting may be validly convened, proper notice must be given to each member entitled to notice[1] in strict accordance with the standing orders or rules of the body, organisation or society affected, and such notice must be issued by the proper officer, person or authority. Where the rules do not specify how much notice must be given, a reasonable notice must be given which will give those whose duty or right it is to attend the opportunity to do so.[2] If a practice grows up of giving a certain length of notice, this will be held to be reasonable in the absence of any particular circumstance which would make such a conclusion invalid.

The requirement for notice does not arise in some cases. Certain bodies, for

---

1 The membership entitled to attend will sometimes be so large that, if all members attend, no single venue could accommodate them: see *British Actors' Equity v Goring* [1978] ICR 791, at 794 (27,000 entitled to notice). This does not alter the obligation to give notice to each.
2 *MacLelland v NUJ* [1975] ICR 116.

instance, hold their meetings on specified days or dates and at specified times and places. Committees of local councils usually fix their meetings for the year shortly after the annual elections; many companies have board meetings fixed in advance. In some cases the practice grows up of sending out no notice, or of only giving notice at the beginning of each year or session of meetings which will be held in that period. Such a practice is valid, unless, of course, it contravenes specific requirements of the regulations of the body concerned.

(1) Notice must (in the absence of provisions to the contrary) be given to every person entitled to attend

The omission to summon one member to a corporate meeting avoids the acts of that meeting.[3] In *Dobson v Fussy*,[4] the question arose whether certain persons were duly assembled as a select vestry. The meeting was held on an unusual day, and no notice was given to one of the members of the select vestry. The court accordingly held that the members were not duly assembled as a select vestry.

A public body entrusted with the performance of a public duty cannot hold an extraordinary meeting unless all the members be summoned who can be summoned, or the unsummoned members are actually present at such meeting. The proceedings at a meeting at which any individual is not present who might have been summoned and was not summoned are void, though the omission be accidental, or though the individual has given a general notice that he or she wishes not to be summoned[5] or the convening officer believed that a certain member was out of the summons.[6] It is competent, however, as, for example, in the case of companies, for the relevant rules to provide that certain classes of members need not be given notice of certain classes of meetings, and also that accidental omission to give a member notice of a meeting is not to invalidate the proceedings at that meeting. The right of an enemy at common law or under the Trading with the Enemy Act 1939 to be given notice of meetings of a company of which he or she is a member is suspended, and a meeting is properly held even though no notice has been given to such a person.[7]

In many cases, provision is made for notice to be given by advertisement, and this is effective. Such advertisement may be required to be inserted in a newspaper or posted in some specified place. If the requirement is complied with, notice is duly given. This is of particular advantage where the persons entitled to notice are unknown, such as holders of bearer warrants, or are all the parishioners in a parish or some such body.

---

3 *R v Mayor, etc of Shrewsbury* (1735) cas *temp* Hardw 147.
4 (1831) 7 Bing 305.
5 *R v Langhorne* (1836) 6 N&M 203.
6 *R v Mayor, etc of Shrewsbury* (1735) cas *temp* Hardw 147.
7 *Re Anglo-International Bank Ltd* [1934] Ch 233.

(2) Notice is not essential if all entitled to attend are present

If all the persons entitled to attend are present and agree to what is proposed, the proceedings cannot afterwards be invalidated on the ground of lack of notice. 'The Court would never allow it to be said that there was an absence of resolution when all the shareholders have expressly assented to that which is being done.'[8] The same principle applies to all meetings.

(3) Absence beyond reasonable summoning distance (or possibly due to serious illness) of a person entitled to attend a meeting may sometimes be a good reason for not summoning that person

> 'The election being by a definite body on a day of which, till summons, the electors had no notice, they were all entitled to be specially summoned, and if there was any omission to summon any one of them, unless they all happened to be present, or unless those not summoned were beyond summoning distance (as, for instance, abroad), there could not be a good electoral assembly, and even a unanimous election by those who did attend would be void.'[9]

In *Re Portuguese Consolidated Copper Mines*,[10] a director of a company, on being told a meeting would be held next week, said, 'I cannot be there'. It was held that this could not be relied on as a waiver of his right to notice, and as no notice was sent to him the meeting was declared invalid. 'Perhaps if a member were at such a distance that it would be absolutely impossible for him to attend, then the secretary might be excused from sending a notice to him and the meeting would be properly convened. Possibly the same exception might hold good when a member was so dangerously ill that he could not be moved.'[11]

It is desirable to send notices of meetings to all members in all circumstances, even to those who may be abroad, since it enables them to be kept fully informed of what is being done at meetings of bodies of which they are members.

In cases where the relevant rules so provide, it is essential to the validity of a meeting that a notice should be sent to a member even though it cannot possibly reach that member until after the meeting has taken place.

(4) Special procedural requirements

Sometimes the constitution of the body in question will require a special procedure to be followed before certain types of meeting may be convened.

---

8 *Re Express Engineering Works* [1920] 1 Ch 466.
9 *Smyth v Darley* (1849) 2 HLC 789 at 803.
10 (1889) 42 ChD 160.
11 *Young v Ladies' Imperial Club* [1920] 2 KB 523. If a meeting may legitimately be summoned in an emergency, it may be enough for those convening it to serve notice on all members who can with proper effort be found: *MacLelland v NUJ* [1975] ICR 116 at 135.

The purpose of such requirements may be to give prominence to matters of particular importance, or to safeguard the interests of the members. Such requirements must be observed if the meeting is to be properly convened. In *MacLelland v NUJ*,[12] the rules of a trade union provided for monthly branch meetings and went on to permit a branch to instruct all its members to attend a 'mandatory' meeting if a motion to this effect was carried at a previous branch meeting. It was held that, without such a motion, no mandatory meeting could be convened, even if a branch meeting had agreed to call such a meeting, for there had to be a motion to instruct all members to attend. Further, the branch meeting had been briefly adjourned to give instructions to those members available to attend a mandatory meeting immediately. It was held that there was only one meeting, the original branch meeting; there had therefore been no 'previous' meeting at which the required motion could be said to have been carried.

(5) Notice should normally state the nature of the business

The notice convening the meeting should, in most cases, contain a sufficient description of the nature of the business which the meeting is to transact, and the meeting cannot in ordinary cases go outside the business described in that notice.[13]

In some cases the practice is not to give any indication of the nature of the business, unless there is something unusual to be considered. For example, notices of meetings of directors in many companies contain no agenda.

In other cases, statute may specify what information should be given. Thus, in *Smith v Deighton and Billington*,[14] the following passage occurs:

'Undoubtedly it was the intention of the Legislature in framing this Statute to provide that due information should be given to all the parishioners of the special purpose for which their attendance is required. ... As to the second part of the resolution – the making a rate for the general expenses of the parish – we are all clearly of opinion that the notice was wholly insufficient for that purpose (ie because the notice did not clearly apprise the parishioners of the special purposes for which the meeting was called) and that the provisions of the Statute have not been complied with.'

In other cases the regulations governing the body concerned may provide that the nature of any business to be transacted, other than routine business, must be specified (see Chapter 14 as regards companies under the Companies Acts).

The object of requiring a proper notice of the purposes for which the meeting is to be held is to enable a member to exercise his or her own judgment as to whether to attend. A notice may be good in part and bad in part, and it is

---

12 [1975] ICR 116.
13 *Longfield Parish Council v Wright* (1919) 88 LJ (Ch) 119.
14 (1852) 8 Moore PC 187.

not wholly invalid because it extends to something which cannot be done at the meeting.[15] The heading in a notice of 'Any other business' will generally authorise the transaction of business of a purely formal nature but not business of any substantial importance. In *Young v Ladies' Imperial Club*,[16] it was held that, as the notice of a meeting did not state the object of the meeting with sufficient particularity, it was invalid and consequently the proceedings of that meeting were invalidated.

In the case of meetings of local authorities and other meetings where the business consists of numerous items, the order and nature of business to be transacted is frequently stated on the agenda. It should, as a rule, be circulated with or as part of the notice to the members who are entitled to be present at the meeting, and often the notice and agenda form one document. The agenda should follow some common form, varying with the type of meeting and the business to be transacted. The order in which items of business should be taken is often regulated by standing orders and, if so, should not be departed from unless the chairman, with the consent of the meeting, approves. No business should be placed on the agenda or transacted at a meeting unless it comes within the scope of the notice convening the meeting.

Agenda are often drawn up in the following order:

(1) Appointment of chairman (if there is no regular chairman).
(2) Verification of the correctness of the minutes of the previous meeting.
(3) Matters arising from the previous meeting's minutes.
(4) Correspondence (a précis of ordinary and routine letters; important letters in full).
(5) Reports of committees and/or officers (reports are often given *in extenso*).
(6) Finance (consideration of accounts and financial questions).
(7) Any special business (the nature of which should be specifically and explicitly stated).
(8) Other motions which can properly be brought before the meeting.
(9) General business.
(10) Date of next meeting.

Under general business, an opportunity may be taken to deal with any formal or unimportant matters, such as a resolution to pay a tradesman's bill. If, however, the relevant rules provide that notice must be given of the business to be transacted, no business of any real importance can be transacted under this head unless proper notice of it has been given.[17] In preparing the agenda, care should be taken to include therein all the business to be transacted, with sufficient detail to enable members to grasp what it means.

An agenda should be clear and explicit, and in a summary form. It should

---

15 *Cleve v Financial Corporation* (1873) LR 16 Eq 363.
16 [1920] 2 KB 523.
17 *Longfield Parish Council v Wright* (1919) 88 LJ (Ch) 119.

enable the members to ascertain what matters will be discussed and, if circulated beforehand, give them an opportunity for forming some opinion as to the course which they will adopt at the meeting. A properly drawn up agenda prevents many questions being put to the chair, considerably shortens a meeting, and helps to get the sense of the meeting in an intelligent and expeditious manner. Further, a well-arranged agenda prevents confusion and irritation which may be caused by members speaking on insufficient information. It is generally advisable to consult the chairman of the meeting in preparing the agenda.

If ordinary routine business is being transacted, notes of the decisions arrived at may be made on the agenda, particularly when a wide margin or space is left for that purpose; but it is generally advisable to have a rough minute-book, so that, when necessary, a detailed and more correct record of the proceedings may be taken. The agenda should be filed and kept for reference.

(6) Notices must be explicit

Notices must be frank, open, clear, satisfactory and free from 'trickiness'. A resolution passed on the basis of an unfair or inadequate disclosure of information in the notice is invalid.[18] 'The Court does not scrutinise these notices with a view to exercise criticism, or to find out defects, but it looks at them fairly. I think the question may be put in this form: What is the meaning which this notice would fairly carry to ordinary minds? That, I think, is a reasonable test.'[19]

(7) Notices must give particulars of their timing

A notice should give the place, date and time of the meeting. If one meeting is to be held immediately after another, it is desirable to fix the time of the second meeting when it is thought the first meeting will end, adding the alternative 'or at the conclusion or adjournment of the previous meeting'.

The place at which the meeting is to be held must be one which is accessible to the persons entitled to be present. A majority cannot bind a whole corporation if a minority is deprived of its right of attending the meeting, for example by holding a meeting in a place to which some members have no access or where the place of meeting is so inconvenient or small that it is physically impossible for all to be present. The general rule is that corporate acts must be done at a meeting properly convened, properly constituted, and properly held at a place of meeting at which every member has the right to attend (although this is subject to some exceptions, which are discussed in Part III). The date of the meeting must be sufficiently far ahead to comply with any relevant

---

18 *Kaye v Croydon Tramways* [1898] 1 Ch 358.
19 *Henderson v Bank of Australasia* (1890) 45 ChD 330 at 337.

requirements as to the length of notice for that meeting, and in the absence of any such provisions the notice should be of a reasonable length.

(8) *Adjourned meetings*

A meeting may be adjourned to complete unfinished business; no notice of the adjourned meeting need be given unless the relevant rules otherwise provide, but no business not specified in the notice of the meeting may be transacted at the adjourned meeting. In some cases, however, the relevant rules require a new notice (cf reg 45, Table A, the Companies (Tables A–F) Regulations 1985, SI 1985/805).

(9) *Clear days' notice*

Where the rules specify a particular length of notice but contain no other provision this means that the notice must be given on the set number of 'clear days' before the meeting.[20]

'Clear days' means days exclusive of the day of the notice of service and of the day on which the meeting is to be held, for example, when 14 days' notice is required, notice for a meeting to be held on the 16th of the month must be served on the 1st. It will be necessary in each case to see from the rules when service is deemed to be effected. Thus, in reg 115 of Table A of the Companies (Tables A–F) Regulations 1985, SI 1985/805, service is deemed to have been effected 24 hours after the letter containing the same is posted. Where this applies and notice is being given by post, the notice required to be served on the 1st of the month in the above example would have to be posted on the last day of the previous month, even if that is a Saturday or Sunday.

Similarly the phrase 'not less than 21 days' notice' in s 378(2) of the Companies Act 1985, means 21 clear days' notice, exclusive of the day of service or the day on which the meeting is to be held.

---

20 See *Re Railway Sleepers Supply Co* (1985) 29 ChD 204 and the authorities there cited.

CHAPTER 3

QUORUM AND APPOINTMENT OF CHAIRMAN

Quorum

A quorum, or minimum number of members, must be present at a meeting and, in the absence of any express regulation or special custom, a simple majority of those present must be in favour of the act done or resolution passed.[1] Regulations will almost invariably exist specifying the quorum. However, where there is no express regulation or special custom, the quorum is half of the members and, where the number of members is an odd number, then the quorum is half of the number of members rounded up to the next whole number. So, for example, the quorum required to constitute a valid meeting of a corporation of 13 members would be seven, and the act or resolution of the majority of these seven or greater number will bind the corporation.[2] (A trading corporation frequently acts without a resolution of the company, for example, by its board of directors or by an agent.)

Regulations generally provide for a lesser quorum than this, and so, as soon after the time for which the meeting was convened as that number is present, the meeting may proceed to business. Generally speaking, it will not be competent for a quorum to be fixed at one, for one person cannot normally constitute a meeting.[3] Unless specially provided for, persons represented by proxy cannot be counted as present in forming a quorum, and only those members can be counted towards a quorum who are competent to take part in the business before the meeting.[4]

A quorum having once been constituted, it is occasionally the practice, when the business of the meeting has been properly started, to continue it if it becomes inquorate unless some member objects and calls the attention of the chairman to the absence of a quorum, as is done in the House of Commons. Business transacted after such an objection would generally be invalid. However, in some cases, statute or the rules of the relevant body intervene to

---

1 *Merchants of the Staple of England v Bank of England* (1887) 21 QBD 160.
2 *Hascard v Somany* (1693) Freem KB 504.
3 *Sharp v Dawes* (1876) 2 QBD 26. Companies incorporated with a single member, as provided in the Companies (Single Member Private Limited Companies) Regulations 1992, SI 1992/1699, constitute an exception to this rule.
4 *Yuill v Greymouth Point Elizabeth R Railway Co* [1904] 1 Ch 32.

provide that no business may be transacted if the meeting becomes inquorate. For example, reg 40 of Table A of the Companies (Tables A–F) Regulations 1985, makes such a provision, as does the Twelfth Schedule to the Local Government Act 1972.

With respect to companies, however, see Chapter 15.

Appointment of chairman

If a person is present who has previously been duly elected chairman or has for some other reason a right to take the chair,[5] that person must take the chair. If there is no such person or such person is not present, the election of a chairman is necessary, and it is desirable in such cases that a temporary chairman, who is not a candidate for the chairmanship, should be chosen, merely for the purpose of electing the chairman.

The chairman may be elected for a particular meeting, or annually, or for a fixed period of time, or sometimes for life. There is usually nothing to prevent a person proposing or seconding himself or herself as chairman. Such a person may vote for themselves.

Often there is a deputy-chairman or vice-chairman who takes the chair in the absence of the regular chairman at the appointed time.

Should the chairman and, if there is one, the vice-chairman be absent, it is open to the members present to elect one of their number to the vacancy, who will retain the position even if the laggard chairman or vice-chairman turns up afterwards. Usually, however, the ordinary chairman is allowed a few minutes' grace before another member is elected to the chair. As a matter of courtesy, though not of right, the chairman thus appointed often gives way to the regular chairman upon the arrival of the latter by vacating the chair. This operates as a virtual resignation, since in the absence of specific provision no special formality is required for a chairman to resign.[6]

A chairman should always be punctual and regular in his attendance and, whenever possible, should send notice to the meeting when he is likely to be absent or unavoidably late.

The opening remarks of the chairman should be brief and to the point. He should direct and control rather than lead a meeting.

(1) How elected

A person nominated to take the chair must be duly proposed and, if there is more than one candidate, the decision of the meeting should be taken either by show of hands or, if the relevant rules so provide and a poll is properly demanded, by a poll. The actual putting of the motion for the election of a

---

5 At a public meeting, the organisers will usually have invited a chairman to preside over the meeting.

6 *Cane v Jones* [1981] 1 All ER 533 at 543.

chairman to the vote is generally done by the proposer or secretary. The motion may not be put to the meeting by the person proposed to be elected as chairman, as 'No man can preside at his own election and return himself.'[7]

(2) *Objection to appointment*

Any objection to the nomination of a chairman should be made there and then. If it is not, it will be too late afterwards to attempt to raise the objection. 'It is alleged that there was an irregularity in nominating the chairman; but it appears on a balance of the evidence that he was nominated and seconded. However, Mr Bluck took the chair, and the meeting acquiesced and adopted him as chairman. In this capacity, he was bound to declare, according to his means of knowledge, the sense of the meeting – that is the duty of the chairman.'[8]

Assuming that his appointment is regular and in order, the newly elected chairman then takes the chair.

(3) *Qualifications of chairman*

The chairman is the person responsible for the actual conduct of the proceedings. 'There is not, as far as I know, any case which has ever arisen to guide us in deciding how far the powers of a chairman extend. . . . Public meetings must be regulated somehow; and where a number of persons assemble and put a man in the chair they devolve on him, by agreement, the conduct of that body. They attorn to him, as it were, and give him the whole power of regulating themselves individually. This is within reasonable bounds. The chairman collects, as it were, his authority from the meeting.'[9]

(4) *Duties of chairman*

The chairman should be well acquainted with the statutory rules, standing orders or other relevant rules of the body over which he or she is presiding, and the chairman's decisions must be governed and controlled by them.

The chairman should:

(i) See that the meeting is properly convened in accordance with the rules and properly constituted – ie that proper notice was given; that there is a quorum of members present; and that his or her own appointment is regular and in order.

(ii) Take care that all the requirements of the relevant rules are duly observed.

(iii) See that the items of business are taken in the order set out in the agenda paper, unless that order is altered with the consent of the meeting.

---

7 *R v White* (1867) LR 2 QB 557 at 561.
8 *Cornwall v Woods* (1846) 4 Notes of Cases 559.
9 *Taylor v Nesfield; Wills on Vestries* 29n.

(iv) Take care that due and sufficient opportunity is given to those who wish to speak (and particularly the minority) to express their views on the subject under debate or discussion. Speakers should be called on by name. The chairman has no right to prevent discussion upon a matter which is included in the notice convening a meeting, and the chairman should see that the sense of the meeting is properly ascertained with regard to any question which is properly before the meeting.

(v) Allow no discussion unless there is some motion[10] before the meeting.

(vi) Prevent irrelevant discussion, and forbid a second speech on the same motion except in the case of a proposer, when under the rules the proposer has a right of reply.

(vii) Take the sense of the meeting by putting the motions and amendments in proper form. Unless the relevant rules otherwise provide, voting will be by show of hands in the first place. In the case of elections governed by the common law there is a right to demand a poll. 'The right to demand a poll being, therefore, as it appears to us, by the common law, an incident to the popular election of a person to an office, we think the electors cannot be deprived of it without a special custom of election inconsistent with such right or expressly excluding it by negative terms, viz that no such right exists in the particular parish.'[11] A similar right may exist in the case of meetings of particular bodies if the relevant rules are silent on the point.

The chairman is not necessarily *functus officio* when he or she has declared the result of the voting.[12] Before declaring that a motion is lost or carried, a chairman has a right to have a recount if he or she is uncertain who has voted for or against the motion. The chairman must also decide all emergent questions which necessarily require decision at the time.[13] In the exercise of his or her authority, the chairman must act bona fide, and in the best interests of the meeting. If the chairman is empowered to demand a poll, then the chairman is under a duty to do so if he or she believes that there is a large number of proxies which may reverse the result which has been obtained on a show of hands.[14] The decisions of the chairman, even when not strictly correct, will be upheld by the court, unless there is evidence that some substantial injustice has arisen from the decisions or that they were not made in good faith.

In *Ex parte Mawby*,[15] where a chairman of a vestry meeting rejected votes

---

10 Ie a proposition for debate, which becomes a resolution if approved. The words 'motion' and 'resolution' are often interchanged when used. The Companies Act 1985, for example, simply refers to 'resolutions', whether passed or merely proposed.

11 *Campbell v Maund* (1836) 5 A&E 865.

12 *Hickman v Kent and Romney Marsh Sheepbreeders' Association* (1920) 36 TLR 528; affirmed (1921) 37 TLR 163.

13 *Re Indian Zoedone Co* (1884) 26 ChD at 77.

14 *Second Consolidated Trust Ltd v Ceylon etc Estates Ltd* [1943] 2 All ER 567.

15 (1854) 3 E&B 718.

which were admissible, but such rejection caused no difference in the result, the court declined to interfere; and in *Shaw v Thompson*,[16] although the court held that the conduct of the chairman was erroneous and illegal, it refused to declare the election null and void, on the ground that there was no evidence that the poll was improperly conducted or that any voter was prevented from recording his or her vote.

As to the chairman's powers of preserving order at the meeting, see Chapter 8, and as to the chairman's power to adjourn the meeting in the event of disorder, see Chapter 9.

(5) The casting vote

In the absence of express provision, a chairman has no second or casting vote,[17] but this privilege may of course be conferred by the relevant rules which govern the meeting. In any case, the chairman only has a casting vote if there is an equality of votes, which means an equality of valid votes. The chairman may exercise his or her ordinary vote one way and the casting vote another, but the chairman may decline to vote at all, and, in the case of an equality of votes, if the chairman declines to vote, the motion is lost. The chairman may give a contingent or hypothetical casting vote to come into operation if, in the course of subsequent proceedings, it should appear that there has been an equality of valid votes.[18]

Where a chairman has a second or casting vote, and intends to exercise both this vote and his or her ordinary vote, the chairman should give his or her first vote while the other members' votes are being taken and before the result of the voting is apparent. It would be quite wrong for a chairman to reserve his or her votes and give, if the numbers proved uneven, for example eight ayes and seven noes, first to the noes the vote as member, and then the casting vote as chairman. It should be noted, however, that it is common for a chairman to be granted a casting vote only and, thus, to have no right to participate in the original vote. Often this has the effect of disenfranchising the chairman as it is not usually desirable for a chairman who wishes to maintain a reputation for impartiality to exercise the casting vote.

For further details of the chairman's position, see Chapter 15.

---

16 (1876) 3 ChD 233.
17 *R v Chapman* (1706) 6 Mod 152; *Weakley v AUEW* (1975) *The Times*, June 12.
18 *Bland v Buchanan* [1901] 2 KB 75.

CHAPTER 4

CONDUCT OF MEETINGS

Introduction

The conduct of a meeting should be governed by the relevant rules. The nature of the rules depends upon the character of the body holding the meetings, but they should be clear, explicit, and free from any ambiguity. They should be fair and reasonable, and interpreted in an impartial manner. From them the chairman obtains most of his or her power, and, if properly drawn up, they form an invaluable authority to which the chairman can appeal. But the chairman must know the rules and understand their purport and meaning, otherwise it may lead to unnecessary conflict with members of the meeting.

Local authorities can make standing orders for the regulation of their proceedings provided they are not inconsistent with the relevant statutory provisions (see Part IV). Where a standing order is made, the local authority is under a duty to comply with it. Usually some provision is made for the suspension of standing orders but this cannot be done by simply ignoring the standing order; it must be done by special resolution.[1]

Where there are no standing orders or where standing orders are inadequate, then either the practice of the House of Commons or the usual practice of previous meetings may be followed. In a simple case, however, the difficulty may be overcome by the chairman exercising his common sense and bearing in mind that it is his or her duty to ascertain the views of the meeting.

Rules should safeguard the general rights of the members of the meeting and should not crush the rights of minorities. When once agreed to, any alteration to the rules should be made only after proper notice has been given to the persons concerned – in fact, there should be a standing rule that any such alteration should require notice of a definite length or should take place only at certain meetings.

Standing orders are of great assistance to chairman, members, and officials alike; they prevent misapprehension of the powers of the meeting, avoid confusion and disorder, and facilitate the dispatch and conduct of business.

Some societies adopt the rules of the House of Commons, *mutatis mutandis*, but these are somewhat complex and unworkable for ordinary meetings.

---

1 *R v Hereford Corporation, ex p Harrower* [1970] 1 WLR 1424.

'It appears to me that meetings of this kind (ie of a limited company) are not bound to model all their proceedings on the rules of the House of Commons. Those rules are very useful; they are the result of long experience, and when those rules are understood they work out admirably. But they are too complex for the apprehension of ordinary shareholders. ... I think the chairman is not to be caught suddenly by an expression of opinion, when he, without very much experience (of course, I am speaking of chairmen in general, not of this chairman), on the spur of the moment, has to come to some conclusion upon some proposal before the meeting; and I am prepared to hold – and do hold – that he is allowed to express his opinion in a deliberate way.'[2]

It is not necessary that a member should persist in disputing the chairman's decision thus given in order to entitle the member to impeach afterwards the validity of such ruling. If the chairman improperly deprives a member of a right to which the member is legally entitled, the validity of the proceedings may be afterwards impeached.

The meeting open to all the members of any particular body is generally the ultimate authority for all the business transacted by that body. Unless there is an express or statutory delegation of authority to a committee or some other body, no reports or resolutions of delegated bodies are binding until they have been confirmed by the delegating body. In some cases, however, much of the important business is often delegated to committees.

Committees

A committee may consist of one person but normally consists of several. 'A committee means a person or persons to whom powers are committed which would otherwise by exercised by another body.'[3] It exercises limited powers, which may be modified or withdrawn by its appointing authority. Its decisions are usually in the form of recommendations which require the adoption or approval of its appointing authority. A committee may, however, be given power to act on behalf of the whole body, and not merely to make recommendations. A committee may, and is sometimes required to be, set up by a local authority to deal with particular subjects. In committee, the proceedings are less formal, and discussion tends rather to elucidate the opinions of the members, and so to form some *consensus ad idem*. The powers of committees should be clearly set forth in their appointment. The chairman and the members of a committee are normally members of the appointing body. It is competent for a particular body, if its rules so provide, to delegate most of the powers to a committee in such a way that those powers can no longer be exercised by the delegating body. Such delegation is generally made by

2 *Henderson v Bank of Australasia* (1890) 45 ChD 330.
3 *Re Taurine Co* (1883) 25 ChD 132.

companies to their boards of directors. In such cases, unless the articles provide otherwise, the exercise by the directors of the powers delegated to them cannot be controlled by the company in general meeting, and to enable the company to do this, it would be necessary to alter the articles (see Chapter 12).

In turn, the committee may appoint sub-committees to deal with some specific branch of its work. A sub-committee stands in the same relation to the committee as the committee does to the whole body of persons by which it is appointed, and can only act within the limits prescribed by its appointing authority, ie the committee. Delegating to a sub-committee does not imply a parting with the powers granted by the delegating committee, but confers an authority to do things which otherwise the committee would do itself. Such powers delegated to the sub-committee can be resumed at any time by the appointing committee.[4] A sub-committee must report to the committee; the existence of a sub-committee expires with the existence of its creating body.

A committee may come into existence and have certain powers even without being expressly appointed. In such a case the powers and jurisdiction of the committee will be implied. An example of such a committee, and the limits on its jurisdiction, is found in the trade union case of *Abbott v Sullivan*.[5]

In some cases a body has no power to delegate. It may also be that the rules of a body, or the contract between the members of a body, may exclude the power to delegate, as in *Bonsor v Musicians Union*[6] where a power delegated to a committee was purported to be exercised by the secretary of the committee and such exercise was invalid and void, since the committee had no power to delegate its authority to the secretary.

A delegating body may also at any time revoke the power of a single member of a committee and that member's appointment to such committee.[7] Revocation of the powers of a committee or of any of its members may be made arbitrarily and even capriciously.[8]

Standing orders

Local authority standing orders[9] will usually deal with, amongst other things, the following matters:

(1) Place, day and time of meetings.
(2) The order of business.
(3) Motions.
(4) Questions.

---

4 *Huth v Clarke* (1890) 25 QBD 391.
5 [1952] 1 KB 189.
6 [1954] Ch 479.
7 *Manton v Brighton Corporation* [1951] 2 KB 393.
8 Ibid.
9 *Model Standing Orders: Contracts* (3rd edn) (HMSO, 1993).

(5) Rules of debate.
(6) Disorderly conduct.
(7) Rescission of resolutions.
(8) Voting.
(9) Appointment of committees.
(10) Suspension of standing orders.

Discussion and debate

The conduct and control of the discussion or debate is mainly in the hands of the chairman, who should be impartial in its management. The following practices are, it is suggested, appropriate:

(1) Every member who so desires should, where practicable, have an opportunity of speaking upon each motion; no second speech should be allowed except that the mover of the original motion should have a right of reply. Every speech should be addressed to the chairman in his or her capacity as chairman. Every member who speaks should direct their speech strictly to the motion under discussion, or to an explanation, or to a question of order. Sometimes a time-limit on the length of speeches is fixed, which may be varied with the consent of the meeting.

(2) The order in which members should speak is determined by the chairman, who should endeavour to ascertain either the implied or express wishes of the meeting on this matter, any conflict of opinion being settled by vote of the meeting. The chairman should call each member who wishes to speak in turn and by name. According to custom, the member who is entitled to address the meeting is the one who first rises to speak or otherwise indicates a desire to speak and who is observed by the chairman; in that event, to prevent uncertainty, the chairman announces the member's name. If a meeting declines to accept the choice of the chairman as to who shall speak, for example, when several members simultaneously indicate a desire to address the meeting, it is open to the meeting to resolve this matter by formal motion (for example, that Mrs A be now heard). However, deference to the chairman is a principle which should be observed. Furthermore, it is not open to the majority to prevent the views of the minority being put forward.[10]

(3) The chairman should impartially allow supporters and opponents of the motion equal opportunities of speaking, and have regard to the rights of minorities.

(4) The chairman should insist on members refraining from unseemly interruptions or making a running commentary on the remarks of the speaker. Similarly the holding of private conversations sotto voce during the

---

10 *Constable v Harris* (1824) T&R 496; *Wall v London and Northern Assets Corporation* [1898] 2 Ch 480.

debate, or any other conduct tending to disturb the meeting should be prevented by the chairman. The chairman should call a member to order for repetition, unbecoming language, or any other breach of order, and may direct such member, if speaking, to discontinue his or her speech.

(5) Points of order which may be raised by any member, whether the member has previously spoken or not, should be taken as soon as they are brought to the notice of the chairman. Explanations, which should be brief and to the point, must not introduce new topics. The chairman should not allow a speech or debate to follow an explanation. The chairman's decision on points of order is final.

(6) Discussion must be relevant to the subject under debate. Members who ignore this rule, or who use offensive language, or impute improper motives to colleagues, should be cautioned by the chairman, and, in the event of persistent disregard of the authority of the chair, should be requested to retire from the meeting, and, if necessary, be removed from the meeting.

These rules are appropriate for private meetings of members entitled to attend and participate. Broadly similar principles should, it is thought, be applied at a public meeting on premises to which admission is controlled by the organisers of the meeting. But at such a meeting the chairman's position, although no more and no less important, is probably stronger. Since (unless granted by the terms of admission) there is no entitlement for those admitted to the meeting to speak, the chairman will have complete discretion in deciding who may address the meeting. The chairman, in such circumstances, has no absolute duty to ensure that everyone who desires to speak is given an adequate chance to do so. However, if the chairman uses his or her discretion arbitrarily, the purpose of the meeting may be undermined.

CHAPTER 5

MOTIONS (OR RESOLUTIONS) AND VOTING

Introduction

A motion, as its name implies, is a proposal moved by a member. If resolved upon, it becomes a resolution. It is common, however, to see reference made to the submitting, proposing or moving of a resolution; for example, in Part XI of the Companies Act 1985.

All motions should be:

(1) In writing, signed by the mover, and handed to the chairman of the meeting, unless they are procedural motions (see below). Every motion and, if successful, the resulting resolution should begin with the word 'That', and should generally be affirmative, not negative,[1] in form.

(2) Relevant to the business for which the meeting is called, within the scope of the notice convening the meeting, and within the powers of that meeting.

(3) Duly proposed and, where it is the practice of the meeting or is required by the rules, seconded.

(4) In compliance with any particular requirements of the relevant rules.

In the House of Commons a motion or amendment does not require to be seconded. The Speaker habitually acts on the mover's proposal of a motion or of an amendment without calling for a seconder and also puts of his or her own accord questions to the House. Where the relevant rules do not otherwise provide, it will be sufficient if the motion or amendment is moved but not seconded, or if the chairman puts a proposal to the meeting.[2]

Motions are in the control of the meeting, and cannot be withdrawn without the unanimous consent of the members present. Motions which are not moved by the person who has given notice of the motion, or by some other member on that person's behalf, are dropped motions and cannot be revived without a new notice. Motions should be discussed in the order in which they appear on the agenda paper, unless the members present wish otherwise. In case of conflict of opinion, the question should be decided by vote.

When there is no amendment to a motion, it is put to the meeting for its

---

1 A negative form is appropriate to reverse a previous commitment by the body in question.
2 *Re Horbury Bridge Coal Co* (1879) 11 ChD 109.

opinion and, if agreed to, becomes the resolution of the meeting. When there is an amendment to the motion, it should be put to the meeting first; if not carried, other amendments in turn may be put, and if all amendments are lost the original motion is put to the meeting for its decision. A mover of a motion is not tied by his or her original motion and may vote for an amendment of the motion. By doing so the mover will in effect withdraw at least pro tanto the original motion.

A resolution rescinding a former resolution passed at a previous meeting is governed by the same principles as any other resolution but sometimes the relevant rules prohibit the rescission of a resolution for a certain period.

Amendments

Unless the relevant rules otherwise require, ordinary amendments can be moved before a vote on the original motion without previous notice, provided they are relevant to the motion, not outside the scope of the notice convening the meeting, and do not involve such a substantial alteration of the motion as to make it a new motion. See, however, Chapter 15 for the position in the case of company meetings.

Amendments generally seek to do one or more of the following things:

(1) To omit certain words.
(2) To omit certain words and insert others.
(3) To insert certain words.

Amendments should be dealt with separately and should be taken in their logical order. The effect of one or more amendments being carried will be to alter the original motion, which should then be put to the meeting again as altered without being again proposed or seconded. If this substantive motion is not carried, no resolution results. It would not, of course, be necessary to put the original motion more than once unless it were altered by amendment.

Amendments are a frequent source of trouble to the chairman. If the chairman is uncertain whether an amendment is in order, the chairman should allow it to be moved so as to save the resolution, since failure to admit germane and relevant amendments will nullify a resolution. In one case, where the chairman's refusal to put the amendment had withdrawn a material and relevant question from the meeting, the court set aside the resolution passed thereat.[3]

Chairmen sometimes refuse to admit amendments on the ground that they have not been seconded, but, unless standing orders expressly provide, the chairman has no alternative but to allow the amendment to be put. 'In my opinion, if the chairman put the question *without its being proposed or seconded by anybody*, that would be perfectly good.'[4] Of course, the mere fact of there

---

3 *Henderson v Bank of Australasia* (1890) 45 ChD 330.
4 *Re Horbury Bridge Coal Co* (1879) 11 ChD 109.

being no seconder may indicate that it is the amendment of a small minority and will therefore be lost.

An amendment:

(1) Must not merely negative the motion. A person wishing to move such an amendment can achieve the same result by voting against it.
(2) Should, if the rules so provide, be formally moved and seconded.
(3) Must come strictly within the scope of the notice convening the meeting. Amendments substantially altering the motion cannot usually be put without proper notice. 'How is it possible for the court to know how many shareholders abstained from attending the meeting, being satisfied that the arrangement, *as it was proposed,* was advantageous to them, and being quite content to exercise no voice about it?'[5] Any amendment without notice which substantially alters the motion of which notice is required is out of order, as is also any amendment which is merely obstructive or dilatory.
(4) Should preferably be in writing, clearly stating the proposed alteration, signed by the mover, and given to the chairman.
(5) May be moved and seconded by members who have not already spoken on the motion, after which all members have a right to speak, unless the relevant rules otherwise provide.
(6) Must not be moved after the question is put.
(7) Gives no right of reply to the mover.
(8) Cannot be withdrawn without the consent of the meeting.
(9) Is deemed not carried if there is an equality of votes, and the chairman does not exercise the casting vote (in the same way as a motion requiring to be passed by a simple majority).

No member can move more than one amendment to the same motion, unless the rules otherwise provide. The meeting must not be asked to vote on two or more amendments at the same time. The chairman should, therefore, allow only one amendment to be before the meeting at a time. When several amendments are before the meeting, it is generally the practice to take them in the order in which they will affect the main question, and not in the order they were moved. It is, however, usual not to allow an amendment of an amendment. If an amendment of an amendment is allowed, it generally leads to confusion. No amendment should be allowed relating to those parts of an original motion which have already been agreed upon as forming part of the amended motion. If the amendment is not carried, the original motion remains to be further amended or discussed.

When an amendment has been put to the meeting and carried, it must be put a second time, embodied in a substantive motion, which supersedes the original motion. This substantive motion can be amended and discussed as if

---

5 *Clinch v Financial Corporation* (1868) LR, 5 Eq 481. Compare *Betts & Co Ltd v MacNaghten* [1910] 1 Ch 430.

it were the original motion. Any amendment which so amends the substantive motion that it becomes again the original motion should not be allowed. It sometimes happens that where an amendment has been carried the substantive motion incorporating that amendment is lost, in which case the original motion is not revived. This is a device which is used to get rid of the whole subject under discussion.

It is not essential to follow the rules of the House of Commons in dealing with amendments. The observance of strict formality in putting motions and amendments thereon to meetings at which there is no recognised practice is unnecessary; it is enough if conflicting propositions are put to the meeting in such a way that those present understand what it is that they are called on to decide.[6]

Amendments when motion is withdrawn

Sometimes a motion to which an amendment is proposed is withdrawn, and if it is properly withdrawn (usually requiring the consent of the meeting), the amendment, ipso facto, falls to the ground and can no longer be moved. But if the original motion could have been moved without notice, a new motion incorporating the amendment, if it is one not requiring notice either, can be moved.

Procedural motions

When a motion has been duly moved and seconded, discussion thereon may be interrupted by motions for amendment (see above) or by some or all of the following further motions, no notice of which is required and which need not be in writing.

(1) To move the previous question (That the question be *not* now put).
(2) To proceed to the next business.
(3) To move the closure (That the question be now put).
(4) To adjourn the debate.
(5) To adjourn the meeting.
(6) To refer a recommendation of a committee back for further consideration and report.

(1) To move the previous question

When the main question, but not an amendment thereto, is under discussion, it is competent for any member who has not spoken on the main question to move the 'previous question', in order to get rid of a motion which is considered inconvenient or on which it is thought unwise for any decision to be taken. If duly seconded, discussion may follow. The 'previous question' is a

---

6 *Ex parte Stevens*, in *Re The Vestry of Hammersmith* (1852) 16 JP 632.

device for shelving the matter for the time being. It raises a question which must be resolved before the main question is considered. The previous question takes precedence over all amendments, and may take the form of 'That the question be now put'; in which case the supporters of the previous question vote against it, and, if successful, the main question is thus got rid of as regards that meeting. The more general way of putting the previous question is in the form: 'That the question be not now put.' If this motion is not carried, the main question is then put to the vote at once without further discussion. On the other hand, if it is carried, the main question cannot be put at that meeting, although it may be brought up at a subsequent meeting. No amendment may be moved to the previous question, though it may be superseded by a motion for adjourning the meeting.

(2) To proceed to the next business

The motion to proceed to the next business, which has the same effect and object as the previous question, that is, to prevent a decision being obtained on the motion under discussion, may generally be moved at the close of any speech, and, if seconded, is put forthwith without speech or debate. If carried, the subject under discussion drops;[7] if lost, there is generally a limit of time, for example half an hour, before this motion can be moved again concerning the same subject of debate.

(3) To move the closure

The motion to move closure is generally moved in the form: 'That the question be now put.' This is moved and put in the same way as the preceding motion. If carried, the motion under discussion is put to the vote. The object of this motion may be either to stifle discussion or to get a decision on a question which has been reasonably or sufficiently debated.

> 'As to the closure, I think if we laid it down that the chairman, supported by a majority, could not put a termination to the speeches of those who were desirous of addressing the meeting, we should allow a small minority, or even a member or two, to tyrannize over the majority. The case has been put ... as the terrorism of the majority. If we accepted this proposition, we should put this weapon into the hands of the minority, which might involve the company in all-night sittings. That seems to me to be an extravagant proposition, and in this particular case there seems to have been nothing arbitrary or vexatious on the part of the chairman or of the majority.'[8]

When the views of the minority have been reasonably heard, it is competent

---

7 A less radical form is a motion that the question lie on the table as tabled, which suspends the matter from further consideration but enables it to be revived at once if the meeting subsequently desires.

8 *Wall v London and Northern Assets Corporation* [1898] 2 Ch 469 at 483.

for the chairman, with the sanction of a vote of the meeting, to declare the discussion closed, and to put the question to the vote. Not everyone is entitled to speak who wants to speak, nor should a member be allowed to speak at undue length. The purpose of a meeting is to get things done, to come to a decision on certain matters, and discussion must be relevant, reasonable, and subordinate to the main object of the meeting. It is thought that, unless the relevant rules otherwise provide, the chairman has a discretion whether or not to accept a motion for the closure, which is an antidote to obstruction or delay. The chairman should use it to defeat mere obstructive tactics, but at the same time have regard to the rights of minorities.

(4) *To adjourn the debate*

The mover of the original motion is usually allowed the right of reply to the motion to adjourn the debate, after which no further debate is permitted. It is often the practice to give the person who successfully carries this motion the right of reopening the debate when it is resumed at the same or the next meeting.

(5) *To adjourn the meeting*

The motion to adjourn the meeting may be moved at the close of any speech or conclusion of any business. The mover of the question under debate at the time is allowed some right of reply. If the motion to adjourn is carried, it is usual to resume the debate or business thus interrupted at the next ordinary meeting, unless another time is fixed, but it is desirable to have this point clearly dealt with by the resolution.[9]

If a motion for adjournment of the debate or of the meeting is defeated, it may be moved again after the debate has gone on for a reasonable time.

(6) *To refer the recommendation of a committee back to the committee*

When a motion emanates from a committee whose province it is to make recommendations on certain defined subjects, it is sometimes referred back to the committee for further consideration, having regard to more recent information which may not have reached the committee, or it may be that other circumstances have intervened since the committee met which may render it inadvisable to adopt the recommendation. Further, the recommendation may not meet with the approval of the parent body, which may not possess the requisite knowledge to amend the motion. In any case, it is regarded as more

---

9 A resolution that 'the chairman leave the chair' adjourns the meeting *sine die* or until the next meeting, if meetings are held regularly.

courteous to give the committee an opportunity of submitting another recommendation. Reference back may in some cases be tantamount to rejection, and is a useful method of negativing a recommendation.

Voting

The usual methods of obtaining the sense of a meeting are:

(1) *Voice.* This is only adopted when it is obvious that the meeting is practically unanimous. The chairman in this case usually reads the motion to the meeting, exclaims 'As many as are of that opinion, say "Aye"', and listens to the voices given in the affirmative. Then he or she says 'As many as are of the contrary opinion, say "no"', and pauses to receive the voices given in the negative. By the volume of the voices the chairman judges whether the ayes or the noes are in the majority. Then the chairman announces 'The ayes (or the noes) have it.' This gives an opportunity for anyone present to demand a vote by show of hands.

(2) *By show of hands.* This is generally adopted in the first instance, each person having one vote. Voting by show of hands means the ascertainment of the views of those persons present who are entitled to vote and who in fact do hold up their hands. If the chairman's declaration as to the result is challenged, a second show of hands should be demanded. Generally, the relevant regulations provide that the declaration of the chairman as to the correctness of the result is decisive, and any objection as to its accuracy should be made at once.

(3) *By a division.* That is, a regular count of the members for and against the motion. In this case members separate themselves by going into different rooms or lobbies, the counting of members being delegated to tellers, one or two being appointed for each side of the question.

(4) *By a poll.* That is, providing an opportunity for every member to cast his or her vote.

In the absence of special provisions, a vote will be taken on a show of hands at the end of which it seems that any voter may demand a poll.

'I am clearly of opinion that the demand for a poll must be made at once, as soon as the preliminary show of hands is over. Where an election is taken by a show of hands, the chairman is to form a judgment at once, to the best of his opinion, as to who is elected; and if it is the intention to test his decision in a more formal manner, this must be done at once.'[10]

'The common-law right on that subject is generally understood to be that any voter, however satisfied with the correctness of the declaration on the show of hands, may yet appeal from it to the whole body of electors, and

10 *R v Vicar of St Asaph* (1883) 52 LJ QB 672. See also *R v Thomas* (1883) 11 QBD 282.

keep a poll open till all have had the opportunity of attending to record their suffrages.'[11]

A demand for a poll probably cannot be withdrawn after it has been accepted and the meeting has come to an end.[12] The demand for a poll is an abandonment of the result of voting by show of hands, and the voting proper begins with the poll.[13] The chairman is the proper person to grant a poll and to make the necessary arrangements.

The cases referred to above are all cases of elections governed by the common law, but it is at least likely that a similar right to a poll exists in other cases where voting takes place and where the relevant rules do not deal expressly with the question.

In one case, it was held that it is no objection to the proceedings at an election by a vestry that the chairman directed a poll without first taking a show of hands, although a show of hands was demanded and the poll was not demanded but was objected to.[14]

Declaration of a poll

One of the duties of the chairman is to declare the poll. If no time is fixed for closing the poll, which should be done in all cases, it cannot be closed while votes are coming in. It may be closed a reasonable time after votes have stopped coming in, although if any voter is improperly excluded the poll will be invalidated.[15]

Abstention

When a motion is put to a meeting a person present may take one of three courses. He or she may vote for or against it, or may abstain from voting at all. A person who is present and abstains may affect the result where, for a motion to be passed, there is required to be cast in its favour a proportion of the votes of those present. It is otherwise where the proportion is of those voting. In *Labouchere v Wharncliff*[16] a motion was put which required a two-thirds majority of those present. Of the 117 persons present, 77 voted for, 38 voted against and 2 abstained. The motion was lost.

There is no necessity for any particular formality in recording a vote. 'A man may give his vote in divers ways, either by writing, or by hand, or by voice, or by conduct, for example by nod. The form in which acquiescence is given matters not, if acquiescence be actually indicated.'[17]

11　*R v The Vestry of St Pancras* (1839) 11 A & E 26.
12　*R v Mayor of Dover* [1903] 1 KB 668.
13　*Anthony v Seger* (1789) 1 Hagg Cons at 13.
14　*R v Rector etc of Birmingham* (1837) 7 A&E 254.
15　*R v Lambeth* (1838) 8 A&E 356.
16　(1879) 13 ChD 346.
17　*Everett v Griffiths* [1924] 1 KB 941 at 953.

A second vote on a resolution

When a chairman has not formally declared the result of a vote or is in doubt as to whether his or her declaration is right or wrong, the chairman is entitled to take a second vote on the matter, especially if he or she considers that through some misunderstanding the first vote did not properly represent the sense of the meeting. In *Hickman v Kent or Romney Marsh Sheepbreeders' Association*,[18] the articles governing the association required in the circumstance 12 voting in favour to 4 against before a certain resolution could be properly carried. The chairman, having put the resolution, counted and found 11 in favour and 4 against. As he had not voted himself and was doubtful whether one or two persons had in fact voted, he put the resolution again, and it was carried by 14 to 4. It was objected that 'when the chairman had counted eleven for and four against he declared the motion carried, and he was then *functus officio* and could not validly have a recount. I do not agree. I think that if he had said that the motion was carried but was in doubt as to whether he was right or wrong, he was entitled immediately to have the votes counted again'.[19]

As to the chairman's vote, see Chapter 3.

---

18 (1920) 36 TLR 528; affirmed (1921) 37 TLR 163.
19 *Hickman v The Kent or Romney Marsh Sheepbreeders' Association* (1920) 36 TLR 528, 533.

CHAPTER 6

SPEECHES AND DEFAMATION

Introduction

Speeches made at meetings and reports submitted in connection therewith come under the general law relating to defamation. Generally speaking, a person making statements at meetings or in reports has little to fear from the law of defamation provided that person acts with reasonable care, and avoids making unsupportable attacks on character and reputation.

Two basic principles of defamation law should be noted:

(1) A defamatory statement is one which tends to lower a person in the estimation of right-thinking members of society generally,[1] or which tends to make them shun or avoid that person. It does not necessarily have to expose that person to hatred or contempt.[2]
(2) A defamatory statement may be either libel or slander. Libel is in written or some other permanent form whereas slander is in oral or some other transient form. Defamatory statements made on television and radio are libel rather than slander.

Defences generally

Statements which are at first sight defamatory can often be made with impunity because of the various defences which may be available in libel proceedings.

(1) Justification

The maker of a defamatory statement can plead justification and say that the statement is substantially true and this will generally provide a defence even if the defendant was actuated by malice. It should, however, be noted that the defendant's honest belief that the statement is true is insufficient if he or she cannot prove it is true. Thus, it is a difficult defence to rely upon. However, if a

---

1 *Sim v Stretch* [1936] 2 All ER 1237.
2 *Drummond-Jackson v British Medical Association* [1970] 1 WLR 691.

person has a conviction for a criminal offence, that is proof that he or she has committed that offence.[3]

Section 5 of the Defamation Act 1952 provides that if the defamatory statement contains more than one charge the defence of justification does not fail just because the truth of every charge is not proved, provided the words not proved to be true do not materially injure the plaintiff's reputation having regard to the truth of the remaining charges. *Polly Peck Holdings v Treford*[4] makes a distinction between two situations which may arise under s 5. One situation is where a defamatory statement includes two distinct charges and the other is where the charges are not wholly distinct but have a common sting. In the former situation, if the plaintiff chooses to sue for defamation only in respect of one charge then the defendant cannot bring evidence in respect of the truth of the other charge. However, in the latter situation, the defendant can justify the common sting of the two charges by bringing evidence in respect of the charge of which the plaintiff has not complained.

(2) Fair comment

It is a defence if it can be established that the statement consisted only of fair comment on a matter of public interest. This defence can in turn be defeated by proof that the statement was made maliciously. The following points enlarge upon this defence:

(a) Matters of public interest include, inter alia, the public conduct of everyone taking part in public affairs, the administration of public institutions and local affairs. Normally, the defence is more likely to apply to proceedings of public bodies than to meetings of private bodies such as societies and limited companies, but the conduct of societies and limited companies, whether public or private, can constitute a matter of public interest in some circumstances. Public interest in a matter can arise 'whenever a matter is such as to affect people at large, so that they may be legitimately interested in, or concerned at, what is going on; or what may happen to them or to others'.[5] Thus, a company's conduct towards its employees[6] and the contents of a prospectus issued to the public[7] have been held to be matters of public interest. The defence of fair comment should, it is thought, extend to all prospectuses and any document filed at the Companies Registry for public inspection.

(b) The statement in question must be comment based on true facts and not asserted as fact. The facts upon which the comment is based may be implied from the comment itself or the background to the publication of

---

3 Civil Evidence Act 1968, s 13.
4 [1986] QB 1000.
5 *London Artists Ltd v Littler* [1969] 2 QB 375.
6 *South Hetton Coal Co v North-Eastern News Association* [1894] 1 QB 133.
7 *Lotinga v Edward Lloyd Ltd* (1910) *The Times*, December 5.

the comment. Such facts need not be made explicit in the comment.[8] (If a defamatory statement of fact is made, the only defences available are justification or qualified privilege.) It is not necessary to prove the truth of all the allegations of fact provided that the statement is fair comment in the light of those allegations of fact which are proved (Defamation Act 1952, s 6).

(c) The comment must be fair. The test of fairness is not whether a reasonable person would hold the defendant's view but whether the defendant is 'an honest man expressing his genuine opinion on a subject of public interest'.[9] A comment is not fair if it imputes to the person defamed discreditable or improper motives unless a fairminded person may upon those facts have held that opinion.[10]

(d) Malice defeats the defence of fair comment. Malice may be shown in two ways:

(i) *When the person making the statement does so either without honest belief in its truth, or recklessly, that is, is indifferent as to whether the statement is true or false.* It follows that proof of carelessness, negligence, anger, indignation or even of a 'gross and irrational prejudice' will not suffice if the speaker honestly, albeit irrationally, believed what he or she said to be true.[11] But it also follows that repetition of gossip without a belief in its truth is capable of being malicious. Malice in this sense is wider than the commonly understood notion of malice or spite.

(ii) *When the dominant motive of the person making the statement is an improper or extraneous motive, such as spite or private advantage, unconnected with the duty or interest which gives rise to the privilege.* The plaintiff's burden in this case is a heavy one and success is unlikely unless the plaintiff can show either that there was no honest belief in the truth of the statement (in which case malice of the first type is present) or that the maker of the statement realised that it had nothing to do with the interest or duty on which a privilege is based and was merely seizing the opportunity to drag in irrelevant defamatory matter.

(3) Absolute privilege

Privilege may be absolute, in which case it provides a complete defence even where the defendant is actuated by malice. For example, statements made in the Houses of Parliament or in the administration of justice are absolutely privileged. However, in most other cases, privilege is qualified.

---

8 *Kemsley v Foot* [1952] AC 345.
9 *Slim v Daily Telegraph* [1968] 2 QB 157.
10 *Peter Walker Ltd v Hodgson* [1909] 1 KB 239; *London Artists Ltd v Littler* [1969] 2 QB 375.
11 *Horrocks v Lowe* [1975] AC 135.

(4) Qualified privilege

Where privilege is qualified the statement is protected unless the maker was motivated by malice (see the discussion of malice, above). Qualified privilege may arise under common law or by virtue of statutory provisions.

(a) Common law

Under the common law, qualified privilege applies whenever the person making the statement has an interest, or a legal, social or moral duty to make it to the person to whom it was made, and the person to whom it was made has a corresponding interest or duty to receive it.[12] Reciprocity of interest and duty between the person making the statement and the person to whom it is made is essential.[13] For newspapers to rely on the defence of qualified privilege, they must show that publication is in the public interest and they are fulfilling a duty in publishing. 'No privilege attaches yet to a statement on a matter of public interest believed by the publisher to be true in relation to which he has exercised reasonable care'.[14]

In respect of qualified privilege, unnecessary publication may be evidence of malice (which destroys the privilege), and the publication may be wider than is justified in the circumstances by the privilege.[15] Thus, where a report has been circulated to members of a committee on a privileged occasion, considered and dealt with, its subsequent re-circulation to the committee may not be the subject of qualified privilege unless it can be shown that it was still reasonably necessary for the performance of the committee's functions or those of its members. This will especially be so if, on the occasion of the first publication, the committee decided to withhold further publication of the report and its membership has, in the meantime, changed so that there is, in effect, a new publication to some of the members.[16]

The presence of the press or other third parties at the making of the defamatory statement does not necessarily prove malice. A distinction should be drawn between the following situations:

(i) where the press or other third parties happen to be present at a meeting (in accordance with the regular custom of the meeting) where a defamatory statement is made,[17] or if the maker of the statement calls in a third person, such as his or her solicitor, to hear what he or she says as a reasonable precaution to protect his or her own interests,[18] in which case the defence of qualified privilege will not be lost;

(ii) where the press or other third parties are expressly invited to attend the

---

12 *Adam v Ward* [1917] AC 309.

13 *Watt v Longsdon* [1930] 1 KB 130.

14 *Blackshaw v Lord* [1983] 2 All ER 311.

15 *Cutler v McPhail* [1962] 2 QB 292; *Chapman v Ellesmere* [1932] 2 KB 431.

16 *R v Lancashire County Council Police Authority, ex p Hook* [1980] QB 603.

17 *Pittard v Oliver* [1891] 1 QB 474.

18 *Taylor v Hawkins* (1851) 16 QB 308.

meeting by the person making the defamatory statement,[19] in circumstances where it might have been made in private,[20] in which case the defence of qualified privilege may be lost.

If several persons make the defamatory statement at an occasion protected by qualified privilege the defence is lost only by those against whom express malice is proved.[21] The malice of an agent may make a principal liable, but the malice of a principal will not make an innocent agent liable.[22]

(b) Statutory provisions

Different types of qualified privilege exist under the Defamation Act 1952. For example, qualified privilege attaches to reports of Parliamentary and judicial proceedings. Of particular interest in this context is the qualified privilege which attaches to the publication in a newspaper or broadcast of matters occurring in meetings of specified bodies. However, this privilege will not protect a defendant where there is publication of any matter which is prohibited by law or is not in the public interest.[23]

The publication of statements made in the meetings of some of these bodies are privileged without explanation or contradiction. For others, explanation or contradiction is necessary if requested by the plaintiff.[24] This work is primarily concerned with the latter class of bodies. These bodies include local authorities, commissions of enquiry, lawful public meetings and general meetings of public companies. General meetings of private companies are not included, and defendants must rely on the common law defences of justification or fair comment in respect of any defamatory reports of such meetings.

Companies

In most cases, statements made in a company meeting, in a board meeting and in reports and circulars to the shareholders are protected by qualified privilege. Evidence of malice destroys the privilege.

(1) Meetings

Qualified privilege protects persons making statements in good faith in a company meeting on a subject in which the members are interested, that is, where the person making the statement has an interest or a legal, social or moral duty to make it to the members, and the members have a corresponding duty or interest to receive it; the privilege may be lost if the statement is made

---

19 *Pittard v Oliver* [1891] 1 QB 474.
20 *Toogood v Spyring* (1834) 1 Cr M & R 181.
21 *Longdon-Griffiths v Smith* [1951] 1 KB 295.
22 *Eggar v Viscount Chelmsford* [1965] 1 QB 248.
23 Defamation Act 1952, s 7(3).
24 Ibid, s 7(2); *Kahn v Ahmed* [1957] 2 QB 149.

privately after the determination of the meeting instead of as part of the proceedings.[25] Statements about the auditors, particular employees, or the directors are examples of subjects in which the members are interested.

The general rule as to the presence of outsiders, stated above, applies so that, provided the person making the defamatory statement has not sought the presence of the press or other third parties at the meeting, the privilege is not destroyed merely through their presence.

(2) Reports and circulars

Reports and circulars sent to the members of the company by the company[26] or by some other members[27] are privileged in the absence of malice. In order to ensure that malice will be regarded as absent, those drafting reports and circulars must ensure that they have an honest belief in the truth of the contents and that there is no unnecessary publication.

(3) Board meetings

Directors of a company have a duty to discuss the affairs of their company and they are entitled to discuss the conduct of their officials so long as they do so honestly.[28] Statements made by a director to an official or a member of the company or to the company's solicitor are normally privileged.[29] An example of the way in which this privilege may be lost by unnecessary publication occurred in *Watt v Longsdon*.[30] In this case, it was held that the defendant director was under a duty to communicate to his chairman a letter of complaint about the conduct of the plaintiff employee, but that he was under no duty to communicate the contents of the letter to the plaintiff's wife. Communication to the plaintiff's wife, therefore, destroyed the privilege.

Local authorities

In the absence of malice, statements made to a local authority on a matter with which the authority is competent to deal are protected by qualified privilege. Local authorities are bound by law to exhibit publicly notices convening council meetings (Local Government Act 1972, Twelfth Schedule). These notices are protected by qualified privilege. They must specify with sufficient clarity the purposes for which the meetings are convened, but need not set out any reports which are to be considered at the meetings. Consequently, if a report set out in a notice which is publicly exhibited is defamatory, it will not be

---

25 *Martin v Strong* (1836) 5 A&E 535.
26 *Lawless v Anglo-Egyptian Cotton Co* (1869) LR 4 QB 262.
27 *Quartz Hill Gold Mining Co v Beall* (1882) 20 ChD 501.
28 *Allan v Clarke* (1912) *The Times*, January 17.
29 *M'Gillivray v Davidson* (1934) SLT 45.
30 [1930] 1 KB 130.

protected by the defence of qualified privilege if the public have no interest in receiving the report.[31]

The publication of the agenda for a local authority meeting to the press or to a member of the public, with or without further particulars indicating the nature of any item, is privileged in the absence of malice.[32] This protection is now extended to certain committee meetings of local authorities as well as council meetings.[33]

Parties

There is a distinction between defaming a corporation and defaming its officers.

(1) Companies generally

A company cannot commence proceedings for words which reflect not upon the company but solely upon its individual officers or members.[34] Further, a trading company may only sue for defamation to protect its trading character.[35]

The trading character of a company may be injured by statements made at meetings or in reports. Thus, it may be defamatory to make a statement reflecting on the conduct of a company's trade[36] or on its financial stability.[37]

A company can sue one of its own directors or members for defamation.[38]

(2) Non-trading companies

Non-trading companies are only entitled to sue for defamation if they are not 'governing bodies'. This principle was laid down by the House of Lords in *Derbyshire County Council v Times Newspapers Ltd*, in which a municipal corporation was prevented from pursuing a defamation action on this basis.[39] Governing corporations may therefore only sue where the statement amounts to a malicious falsehood, in relation to which proof of malice is (of course) necessary.[40]

---

31 *De Buse v McCarthy* [1942] 1 KB 156.
32 Public Bodies (Admissions to Meetings) Act 1960, s 1(5); Local Government Act 1972, s 100H, as inserted by Local Government (Access to Information) Act 1985.
33 Local Government Act 1972, s 100.
34 See, further, Patfield 'Protecting the Reputation of Corporate Personnel, Organs and Associates' (1988) 18 *University of Western Australia Law Review* 203.
35 *South Hetton Coal Co v North-Eastern News Association Ltd* [1893] 1 QB 133.
36 *D and L Caterers Ltd and Jackson v d'Anjou* [1945] KB 364.
37 *Irish People's Assurance Society v City of Dublin Assurance Co Ltd* (1929) IR 25.
38 *Metropolitan Saloon v Hawkins* (1859) 4 H&N 87.
39 [1993] 2 WLR 449. See, further, Patfield 'Corporate Public Authorities and Freedom of Speech' (1993) 14 *The Company Lawyer* 98.
40 *Ratcliffe v Evans* [1892] 2 QB 524.

It appears that most non-governing non-trading companies are entitled to sue for defamation, although only where, as with trading companies, the words reflect on the activity of the company rather than merely the individuals who compose it.[41] Special note, however, should be taken of the position of trade unions. A trade union may sue for defamation if, and only if, it is a 'special register' body within the meaning of the Trade Union and Labour Relations (Consolidation) Act 1992.[42] Subject to this, there is no doubt that a union has a reputation which it may protect against injury by proceedings in defamation.[43]

---

41 *Saskatchewan College of Physicians and Surgeons v Co-operative Commonwealth Federation Publishing and Printing Co Ltd* (1951) 51 DLR (2d) 442.
42 *Electrical, Electronic, Telecommunication and Plumbing Union v Times Newspapers Ltd* [1980] QB 585.
43 *National Union of General and Municipal Workers v Gillian* [1948] KB 81.

CHAPTER 7

ADMISSION TO MEETINGS (INCLUDING THE PRESS)

One of the matters which must sometimes be decided in connection with meetings is who should be invited to attend. In the case of a public meeting held in a public place, no one can be excluded. In the case of a public meeting on private premises, however, the organisers can decide who may come to the meeting. Generally speaking, in the case of private meetings, there is no right to attend for the public or press, but the meeting itself may decide whether outsiders of any kind shall be permitted to be present. Large public companies, for example, generally desire that their general meetings shall be reported in the papers, and so invite the attendance of reporters, but they are not bound to do so.

The rights of the public and press to attend meetings of local authorities are governed by the Public Bodies (Admission to Meetings) Act 1960 and the Local Government (Access to Information) Act 1985. The former statute governs the access of the public and press to the meetings of parish and community councils and parish meetings. It provides that the meetings of such bodies should normally be open to the public, but in certain circumstances the public may be excluded by resolution. The Local Government (Access to Information) Act 1985 provides that the meetings of principal councils, joint authorities and their committees and sub-committees should normally be open to the public, but again there are certain circumstances in which the public must or may be denied access to the meetings of such bodies. Both statutes provide that three clear days' public notice of the time and place of a meeting should be given and that duly accredited press representatives should be afforded reasonable facilities for taking their report and for telephoning in at their own expense. For further details of the rights of the public and press to attend the meetings of local authorities, see Part IV.

CHAPTER 8

EXPULSION FROM MEETINGS

When a meeting of a body or society takes place in premises which are private property or to which a stranger has no right of access,[1] a stranger may only remain so long as no objection is made to his or her presence. If the stranger is requested to leave and refuses to do so then he or she becomes a trespasser and may be ejected with such reasonable force as is required. It is unnecessary for these purposes that any reason be given to support the request that the stranger leave.

The expulsion, however, of a member of a meeting (that is, of a person who is entitled to attend that meeting) except for disorderly conduct of a serious nature is illegal unless standing orders otherwise provide, and such standing orders are within the powers of the constitution governing the meeting.

> 'The power, therefore, of suspending a member guilty of obstruction or disorderly conduct during the continuance of any current sitting, is ... reasonably necessary for the proper exercise of the functions of any legislative assembly of this kind; and it may very well be, that the same doctrine of reasonable necessity would authorise a suspension until submission or apology by the offending member; which, if he were refractory, might cause it to be prolonged (not by the arbitrary discretion of the assembly, but by his own wilful default) for some further time.'[2]

Similarly, in *Doyle v Falconer*,[3] it was said that if a member of a colonial House of Assembly was guilty of disorderly conduct in that House while sitting, he might be removed or excluded for a time or even expelled, and that if the conduct of the members was not such as to secure order and decency of debate, the law would sanction the use of that degree of force which might be necessary to remove the person offending from the place of meeting and to keep him excluded, and that the same rule would apply even more so to obstructions caused by a non-member. In either case, if the violation of order amounted to a breach of the peace, recourse might be had to the ordinary courts.

---

1 As to meetings held in a public place, see Chapter 11. It is an offence to use or threaten violence to secure entry into any premises.
2 *Barton v Taylor* (1886) 11 App Cas 197, at 204; a case concerned with the New South Wales Assembly.
3 LR 1 PC 328 at 340.

It is the duty of the chairman to preserve order at the meeting, and consequently, in the event of a member of a meeting being so disorderly as to interfere unduly with the reasonable conduct of the meeting or to prevent the proper transaction of business, the chairman may order that member to withdraw. If the member refuses to comply with this order, he or she may be ejected with reasonable force. If the disorderly member resists ejection, this may constitute a breach of the peace. It is usually desirable, however, that the chairman should be supported by the majority of the meeting before ordering a member to withdraw, and should take care not to give instructions for ejection unless he or she is quite sure such instructions will be expeditiously and efficiently carried out.

It should be noted that the expulsion of a member from the society or club as a whole will, of course, make that member a stranger for the purposes of these roles.

CHAPTER 9

ADJOURNMENTS

The power to adjourn is, in the absence of contrary rules, vested in the meeting itself.[1] If the chairman leaves the meeting before the business is completed, or if the chairman purports to adjourn the meeting without authority, the meeting may, if a quorum still remains, appoint another chairman and proceed with the business. Subject to the following, the chairman has no right to adjourn the meeting without the consent of the meeting itself unless the business for which it was convened has been done or an express power in that behalf is given to the chairman in the relevant rules.[2]

In *Byng v London Life Association Ltd*,[3] the Court of Appeal held that in certain circumstances a chairman has a residual common law power to adjourn a meeting. In this case, the articles of association of the company provided that the chairman only had the power to adjourn if there was consent to adjournment by a quorate meeting. The Court of Appeal held that if, as occurred in the case, it is not possible for the chairman to ascertain the views of the meeting the chairman is entitled to rely upon the residual common law discretion to adjourn. The chairman is only entitled to exercise this discretion if the chairman acts in good faith and takes into account all relevant factors. According to Browne-Wilkinson LJ, a chairman's decision to adjourn will be declared invalid if the chairman 'failed to take into account all relevant factors or reached a conclusion which no reasonable chairman, properly directing himself as to his duties, could have reached.'[4]

In the event of disorder the chairman may rely on the residual discretion to adjourn, provided that the discretion is exercised on the proper basis as described in *Byng v London Life Association Ltd*. An adjournment in the event of disorder must be for no longer than the chairman considers necessary and the chairman must, so far as possible, communicate the decision to adjourn to those present.[5]

Where a meeting is inquorate then, not only does it lack the power to transact business, it also lacks power to resolve upon an adjournment. The

---

1 *Stoughton v Reynolds* (1736) 2 Strange 1044; *R v Grimshaw* (1847) 11 Jur 965.
2 *National Dwellings Society v Sykes* [1894] 3 Ch 159.
3 [1989] BCLC 400.
4 Ibid. See, further, Chapter 19.
5 *John v Rees* [1970] Ch 345.

relevant rules may make provision for such an eventuality. For example, reg 41 of Table A of the Companies (Tables A–F) Regulations 1985, provides that where a quorum is not attained, or ceases to exist, the meeting will be adjourned 'to the same day in the next week at the same time and place or to such time and place as the directors may determine'.

Postponement of meetings

A properly convened meeting cannot be postponed. The proper course to adopt is to hold the meeting as originally intended, and then and there adjourn it to a more suitable date. If this course is not adopted, members will be entitled to ignore the notice of postponement, and, if sufficient to form a quorum, hold the meeting as originally convened and validly transact the business threat.

CHAPTER 10

MINUTES

The minutes of a meeting comprise a record of what was done at the meeting, for example, resolutions and decisions of the meeting should be minuted, but not the speeches or arguments in connection therewith. The minutes may be drawn up during the meeting and put up for approval at the end of the meeting, but the more usual course is to approve them at the next meeting. Any inaccuracy in the minutes is fatal to their value and usefulness.

The minutes should be:

(1) An exact account of what was actually agreed upon.
(2) Sufficiently detailed and complete, so that a member who was absent could fully understand what was done at that meeting.
(3) Concise.

The minutes should contain, inter alia:

(1) In the case of meetings of a local authority and where the meeting is of a comparatively small body, for example, of the board of directors of a company or of a committee, the names of the members present. It is usual in the meetings of small bodies to record in the minutes the names of those persons who vote against a specific resolution, if they request this to be done.
(2) Full and exact details of all contracts and questions involving financial considerations.
(3) The exact words of all resolutions which have been passed.
(4) Appointments, salaries, powers and duties of officials (these should be very explicit).
(5) Instructions to officials, and all transactions authorised at that meeting.

Minutes, when lengthy, should be carefully indexed, and when not in actual use should, if possible, be kept in a fireproof safe. Where the business transacted at a meeting is of some importance, copies of the minutes of that meeting may be circulated with the notice of the next meeting. It is important that the minutes should be signed by the chairman, either of the meeting at which they were taken or of that at which they were verified. It is unwise for a chairman to sign the minutes without getting them verified as correct by a meeting. The usual method is to bring up the minutes at the next succeeding meeting, when they are read if not previously circulated. The chairman then asks whether in the opinion of the meeting they are a correct report of the proceedings, and, if the answer is in the affirmative, the chairman formally signs them. It is not necessary that the chairman should have been present at the meeting at which they were taken. There are certain statutory provisions as to the evidential value of minutes when so signed in the cases of companies and local authorities, and these are discussed respectively in Parts III and IV. The relevant rules may, however, provide that the minutes shall be conclusive evidence of the facts therein stated and such a provision will be good in the absence of fraud.[1]

Any discussion on the minutes, except as to their accuracy, is out of order, and the chairman should rule accordingly. Questions arising out of the minutes are permissible with the consent of the meeting if only for information and not for discussion. If there is a conflict of opinion as to their accuracy, an amendment to the motion of their correctness, embodying the suggested alteration, should be put to the meeting and it is obvious that those who were not present at the preceding meeting should not take part in the discussion or vote. The approval of the minutes by a meeting merely verifies their accuracy; it does not necessarily mean that such minutes are adopted or that the resolutions therein are confirmed or ratified.

---

1 *Kerr v John Mottram* [1940] Ch 657.

PART II

PUBLIC MEETINGS

CHAPTER 11

PUBLIC MEETINGS

Definition of a public meeting

There is no definition of a public meeting in the Public Order Act 1986. Section 9 of the Public Order Act 1936 defines a public meeting as any meeting in a public place which the public or any section thereof are permitted to attend, whether on payment or otherwise. 'Meeting' means a meeting held for the purpose of the discussion of matters of public interest or for the purpose of the expression of views on such matters. 'Public place' includes any highway and any other place to which the public at the material time are permitted to have access, whether on payment or otherwise.

Where meetings may be held

There is no positive right to hold a public meeting. There is a residual freedom to assemble, provided that it is not unlawful to do so.

Public highways

A highway is a way over which there exists a right of passage and repassage. Reasonable use of the highway for purposes incidental to passage is permitted.[1] Thus, stopping to rest or queuing for a bus or entertainment are permissible.[2] However, use of the highway other than for passage and repassage or purposes incidental to passage and repassage, for example holding a public meeting, may constitute a trespass actionable by the owner of the soil of the highway, usually the local authority. Unreasonable obstruction of the highway may also constitute a public nuisance actionable by the Attorney-General or a person who suffers special loss.[3]

It is a criminal offence under s 137 of the Highways Act 1980 for a person without lawful authority or excuse to in any way wilfully obstruct the free passage along a highway. Reasonable use of the highway will constitute an excuse even though an obstruction has been caused. Whether a use is reasonable or not depends upon all the circumstances including the length of time for which

---

1 *Harrison v Duke of Rutland* [1893] 1 QB 142; *Hickman v Maisey* [1900] 1 QB 752.
2 *Hubbard v Pitt* [1976] QB 142.
3 *R v Clark (No 2)* [1964] QB 315.

the obstruction continues, the place where it occurs, the purpose for which it was done, and whether or not it caused an actual or potential obstruction.[4] A person's genuine belief that he or she has lawful authority for what he or she is doing does not mean the obstruction cannot be wilful 'if a person does something intentionally as opposed to accidentally, that is, by an exercise of his or her free will, does something or omits to do something which will cause an obstruction or the continuance of an obstruction he is guilty of an offence.'[5]

Near to Parliament

Section 23 of the Seditious Meetings Act 1817, which made it an offence for meetings of more than 50 people to be held within one mile of Westminster hall during the sitting of Parliament, was repealed by the Public Order Act 1986. However, Parliament has power to regulate access to the Houses of Parliament by directing, at the beginning of each session, the Metropolitan Police Commissioner to keep the streets leading to Parliament open and order that Lords and members do not have their access to Parliament obstructed. The Commissioner enforces the sessional orders by giving directions under s 52 of the Metropolitan Police Act 1839. Section 54(9) of the same Act makes it an offence to wilfully disregard or fail to conform to the directions.

Parks and other public spaces under local authority control

Local authorities may make areas under their control subject to by-laws made under statutory powers. A by-law may prohibit the holding of a public meeting except at a time or place specified by the authority or without the prior permission of the authority. A by-law of such a nature, if made within the scope of a statutory power, is valid. There is no right for the general public to hold meetings on a common.[6]

Premises owned by a local authority

Local authorities may hire out their premises for public meetings. Such an agreement can incorporate the relevant local authority rules governing the conduct of the meeting but in the absence of a clear breach of those rules the local authority has no more power than a private landowner to withdraw from an agreement, for example, if it decides the intended meeting is of an organisation which the authority finds distasteful.[7] Local authorities are under a statutory duty to make certain rooms under their control available free of charge for the holding of election meetings.[8]

---

4 *Nagy v Weston* [1965] 1 All ER 78; *Hirst and Agu v Chief Constable of West Yorkshire* (1986) 85
   Cr App Rep 143.
5 *Arrowsmith v Jenkins* [1963] 2 QB 561.
6 *De Morgan v Metropolitan Board of Works* (1880) 5 QBD 155.
7 *Verrall v Great Yarmouth Borough Council* [1981] 1 QB 202.
8 Representation of the People Act 1983, ss 95 and 96.

Royal Parks and Trafalgar Square

There is no right to hold public meetings in Royal Parks unless regulations so provide.[9] There is no right to hold a public meeting in Trafalgar Square.[10] The Trafalgar Square Regulations 1952 provide that an application to hold a meeting in Trafalgar Square must be made to the Department of Environment. No application will be considered in advance of three months before the proposed meeting. Meetings can be held in Trafalgar Square on Saturdays between 2 pm and sunset, and on Sundays and public holidays between sunrise and sunset.

General conduct

The platform should be carefully planned – sufficient seating should be provided for those who will attend the meeting. Stewards may be employed to help people to their seats and to assist in the preservation of good order.[11]

The chairman, who is normally selected in advance of the meeting by its conveners, should open the meeting with a few brief words of introduction. The order of the meeting should proceed as prearranged. There is no obligation on the part of the chairman to allow anyone to speak or to ask questions. The speakers and the procedure are determined by the chairman and the conveners of the meeting.

Disorder at public meetings

Disorder may arise at a public meeting for any one of many causes. For example, it may be caused by violent or irrelevant interruptions, by organised opposition, or by a weak and tactless chairman.

If a meeting is held on private premises, then those who attend are bound to observe the rules laid down by the conveners of the meeting and subject to their reasonable control. A person who has paid for admission has a contractual licence; a contract containing a permission to occupy the premises for the purpose of the meeting for the duration of the meeting. Where a person with a contractual licence (the licensee) behaves properly, the person who granted the licence is under an obligation not to revoke that licence by ejecting the licensee.[12]

A person who has not paid for admission has a bare licence which can be revoked at any time. Once the licence is revoked, the licensee becomes a trespasser, although he or she must be given a reasonable time in which to

---

9 *Bailey v Williamson* (1873) LR 8 QB 118.
10 *Ex parte Lewis* (1888) 21 QBD 191.
11 Public Order Act 1936, s 2(6).
12 *Hurst v Picture Theatres Ltd* [1915] 1 KB 1; *Winter Garden Theatre (London) Ltd v Millenium Productions Ltd* [1948] AC 173.

leave the property.[13] If after a reasonable interval the licensee refuses to leave, he or she may be removed with use of reasonable force. Use of excessive force will entitle a person to damages.[14]

Those who attend public meetings, whether by payment or otherwise, and who participate in disorder, may be removed from a meeting if their behaviour is such that the police are empowered to act against them (see below).

The powers of the police

The police have powers to deal with a range of criminal offences which may be committed by those who are involved in disorder at public meetings.

Criminal trespass

Section 6 of the Criminal Law Act 1977 makes it an offence for any person without lawful authority to use or threaten violence against another person or against property in order to secure entry to premises on which he or she knows there to be present a person who is opposed to his or her entry. Section 8 of the same Act makes it an offence to trespass on any premises with a weapon of offence ie any article made or adapted, or intended by the person who has it, for use for causing injury to or incapacitating another person. The offences may be committed in relation to part of a building – thus where a hall has been set aside for a meeting to which entry is controlled, members of the public who may have lawful access to the remainder of the building may nevertheless commit an offence by seeking unlawful entry into the hall. For both of the above offences a uniformed police officer may arrest without warrant any person who is, or whom the officer suspects with reasonable cause to be, guilty of the offence.[15]

Public Meeting Act 1908

Section 1 of the Public Meeting Act 1908 provides that any person who at a lawful public meeting acts in a disorderly manner for the purpose of preventing the transaction of the business for which the meeting was called together shall be guilty of an offence. It also provides that any person who incites others to commit the above offence shall be guilty of an offence. If a constable reasonably suspects that an offence has been committed under s 1 of the Public Meeting Act 1908, the constable may, on the request of the chairman, require the person concerned to give his or her name and address. Failure or refusal to give a name and address or giving a false name and address is an offence. The Public Meeting Act 1908 gave the police a power of arrest where

---

13 *Robson v Hallet* [1967] 2 QB 939.
14 *Hawkins v Muff* (1911) *The Times*, March 24.
15 The power of arrest in s 6(6) and s 8(4) was preserved by the Police and Criminal Evidence Act 1984, Sch 2.

a person failed or refused to give his or her name or address or where a constable reasonably suspected that person of giving a false name and address. The power of arrest was repealed by the Police and Criminal Evidence Act 1984 (PACE) and replaced by PACE, s 25 which permits an arrest without warrant where a constable has reasonable grounds for suspecting that an offence has been committed or attempted, or is being committed or attempted, and it appears to the constable that service of a summons is impracticable or inappropriate because any of the general arrest conditions are satisfied.[16]

Representation of the People Act 1983

Section 1 of the Public Meeting Act 1908 does not apply to election meetings, which are governed by s 97 of the Representation of the People Act 1983. Section 97 provides that it is an illegal practice to act or incite others to act in a disorderly manner for the purpose of preventing the transaction of business for which the election meeting was called together. If a constable reasonably believes that an offence has been committed under s 97, the constable may, on the request of the chairman, require the person concerned to give his or her name and address. Failure or refusal to give a name and address or giving a false name and address is an offence. The power of arrest for this offence was repealed by PACE and replaced by PACE, s 25 (see above).

Breach of the peace

The police have powers at common law to prevent a breach of the peace. The police may arrest a person for breach of the peace where a breach is committed in their presence, or where they reasonably believe that such a breach will be committed in the immediate future by the person arrested although he or she has not yet committed any breach, or where a breach of the peace has been committed and it is reasonably believed that a renewal is threatened.[17] Where arrest is for an anticipated breach of the peace, the police must have an honest and reasonably formed opinion that there is a real risk of a breach of the peace in the sense that it is in close proximity both in place and time.[18] A breach of the peace can take place on private premises.[19] The police are entitled to enter and remain on private premises where a meeting is being held if they

---

16 The general arrest conditions are: (a) that the name of the person is unknown to and cannot be readily ascertained by the constable; or (b) the constable has reasonable grounds for doubting whether the name given is correct; or (c) the person has failed to provide a satisfactory address for service; or (d) the constable has reasonable grounds for doubting whether the address is satisfactory; or (e) the constable has reasonable grounds for believing that arrest is necessary to prevent the person causing harm to himself or another, suffering physical injury, causing loss or damage to property, committing an offence against public decency or obstructing the highway; or (f) the constable has reasonable grounds for believing that arrest is necessary to protect a child or other vulnerable person.

17 *R v Howell* [1982] QB 416.

18 *Moss v McLachlan (Charles)* (1985) 149 JP 167.

19 *McConnell v Chief Constable of the Greater Manchester Police* [1990] 1 All ER 423.

reasonably apprehend a breach of the peace.[20] Proof of annoyance and disturbance, for example by cries of 'Hear, Hear', putting questions to the speaker, and making general observations on the speaker's statements are not enough to amount to a breach of the peace.[21]

Imposing conditions upon public assemblies: s 14 of the Public Order Act 1986

Section 14 of the Public Order Act 1986 empowers the police to impose conditions upon public assemblies. By s 16, a public assembly is defined as an assembly of 20 or more persons in a public place which is wholly or partly open to the air. Thus, s 14 does not enable the police to impose conditions upon public meetings which take place entirely indoors, but it does provide the police with new powers to control open-air assemblies. By s 14, if the senior officer of police (the chief constable, or officer of most senior rank at the scene of an assembly) reasonably believes that:

(a) an assembly may result in serious public disorder, serious damage to property or serious disruption to the life of the community; or
(b) the purpose of the persons organising it is the intimidation of others with a view to compelling them not to do an act they have a right to do, or to do an act they have a right not to do, the officer may impose such conditions upon persons organising or taking part in the assembly as to:
   (i) the place where the assembly may be held;
  (ii) the maximum duration of the assembly; or
 (iii) the maximum number of persons who may constitute the assembly as appear to the officer to be necessary to prevent such disorder, damage, disruption or intimidation.

There is no power to ban a public assembly under s 14. It is possible that conditions could be imposed which have the effect of a ban, but any such condition could be challenged by application for judicial review. By s 14(4) and s 14(5) of the Public Order Act 1986, it is an offence for a person who organises or takes part in a public assembly to knowingly fail to comply with a condition imposed, although it is a defence to show that failure arose from circumstances beyond the defendant's control. By s 14(6), a person who incites another to take part in a public assembly and knowingly breach a condition imposed is guilty of an offence.

Public order offences under the Public Order Act 1986

Those involved in disorder at public meetings may commit one or more of the offences in ss 1–5 of the Public Order Act 1986.

---

20 *Thomas v Sawkins* [1935] 2 KB 249.
21 *Wooding v Oxley* (1839) 9 C&P 1.

Riot

The common law offence of riot has been replaced by s 1 of the Public Order Act 1986, which provides that where 12 or more persons who are present together use or threaten unlawful violence for a common purpose, and their combined conduct is such as would cause a person of reasonable firmness present at the scene to fear for his or her personal safety, those persons who use unlawful violence for the common purpose are guilty of riot. 'Violence' includes violence towards property as well as person and there is no requirement for injury to be caused or even intended by violent conduct.[22] There is no need to prove that a person of reasonable firmness was present at the scene. It is sufficient to show that, had such a person been present, he or she would have feared for his or her personal safety. For a person to commit the offence of riot, he or she must actually use unlawful violence for the common purpose. By s 6(1) of the Public Order Act 1986, a person is only guilty of riot if he or she intends to use violence or is aware that his or her conduct may be violent. Proof of intention or awareness can be inferred from the defendant's conduct. Riot is triable only on indictment and the maximum penalty is 10 years' imprisonment and/or a fine.

Violent disorder

The common law offence of unlawful assembly has been replaced by s 2 of the Public Order Act 1986 which creates the offence of violent disorder. Where three or more persons who are present together use or threaten unlawful violence and the conduct of them taken together is such as would cause a person of reasonable firmness present at the scene to fear for his or her personal safety, those persons using or threatening unlawful violence are guilty of violent disorder. It is not necessary for three persons to be convicted of violent disorder, one or two may be convicted provided that it is proved that three or more persons present together were using or threatening unlawful violence.[23] As with riot, 'violence' includes violence towards property as well as persons and there is no requirement for injury to be caused or even intended by the violent conduct. Again, the person of reasonable firmness is purely hypothetical and there is no need to prove the presence of such a person at the scene. Unlike the offence of riot, violent disorder is committed when a person uses *or threatens* unlawful violence. By s 6(2) of the Public Order Act 1986, a person is guilty of violent disorder only if he or she intends to use or threaten violence or is aware that his or her conduct may be violent or threaten violence. Violent disorder is triable either way and is punishable with a maximum of five years' imprisonment and/or a fine on indictment or six months' imprisonment and/or a fine on summary conviction.

---

22 Public Order Act 1986, s 8.
23 *Mahroof* (1988) 88 Cr App Rep 317; *Fleming* [1989] Crim LR 658; *Worton* [1990] Crim LR 124.

Affray

The common law offence of affray has been replaced by s 3 of the Public Order Act 1986 which provides that a person is guilty of affray if he or she uses or threatens unlawful violence towards another and his or her conduct is such that a person of reasonable firmness present at the scene would fear for his or her personal safety. 'Violence' does not include violence towards property.

There is no requirement for injury to be caused or intended by the violent conduct. A threat of unlawful violence cannot be made by words alone; for the offence of affray to be committed, words must be accompanied by a physical gesture, for example shaking a clenched fist. As with the offences of riot and violent disorder, the person of reasonable firmness is purely hypothetical and there is no need to prove the presence of such a person at the scene. When violence is limited to those involved and others present do not fear for their personal safety then it may be that no offence is committed under s 3.[24] By s 6(2), a person is guilty of affray only if he or she intends to use or threaten violence or is aware that his or her conduct may be violent or threaten violence. Affray is triable either way and is punishable with a maximum of three years' imprisonment and/or a fine on indictment or six months' imprisonment and/or a fine on summary conviction.

Threatening behaviour

The offence of threatening behaviour under s 5 of the Public Order Act 1936 has been replaced by s 4 of the Public Order Act 1986, which provides that a person is guilty of an offence if:

(a) he or she uses towards another person threatening, abusive or insulting words or behaviour; or
(b) he or she displays to another person any writing, sign or other visible representation which is threatening, abusive or insulting

and

(a) he or she intends that person to believe that immediate unlawful violence will be used against him or her or another by any person; or
(b) that person is likely to believe such violence will be used; or
(c) he or she intends to provoke the immediate use of unlawful violence by that person or another; or
(d) it is likely that such violence will be provoked.

The new offence is not restricted to situations where a person is likely to be provoked to violence. (Under s 5 of the Public Order Act 1936, difficulties had

---

24 *DPP v Cotcher* (1992) *The Times*, December 29.

arisen where the 'that person' was unlikely to be provoked, for example because of age or status.[25]) The offence is also committed where a person fears unlawful violence will be used. The words 'threatening', 'abusive' and 'insulting' appeared in s 5 of the Public Order Act 1936 as well as s 4 of the Public Order Act 1986, therefore guidance to their meaning can be derived from cases under the 1936 Act. Words or behaviour do not need to be threatening, abusive *and* insulting; it suffices that they fall under one of these heads. The words threatening, abusive and insulting are to be given their ordinary meaning.[26] Insult means to 'hit by words'; a speaker must take his audience as he finds them, thus an audience which contained Jews was insulted by assertations by the speaker that 'Hitler was right'. It made no difference that the audience might not have been insulted had it consisted solely of the speaker's supporters.[27]

The words 'towards another person' in s 4 of the Public Order Act 1986 mean in the presence of and in the direction of that other person.[28] The offence under s 4 can be committed in a public or private place, but not inside a dwelling.[29] For the offence to be committed, the threatening, insulting or abusive words, behaviour, writing, sign or other visible representation must be intended or be likely to provoke *immediate* unlawful violence.[30] By s 6(3), a person is only guilty of an offence under s 4 if he or she intends his or her words or behaviour or writing, sign or other visible representation to be threatening, abusive or insulting or is aware that it may be threatening, abusive or insulting. The offence is triable only summarily and it is punishable with a maximum of six months' imprisonment and/or a fine.

Harassment, alarm or distress

By s 5 of the Public Order Act 1986, a person is guilty of an offence if:

(a) he or she uses threatening, abusive or insulting words or behaviour; or
(b) he or she uses disorderly conduct; or
(c) he or she displays any writing, sign or other visible representation which is threatening, abusive, or insulting, within the hearing or sight of a person likely to be caused harassment, alarm or distress thereby.

The offence is much wider than the s 4 offence because it covers behaviour which neither provokes nor leads a person to believe violence will be used. The comments upon the meaning of the words 'threatening', 'abusive' and

---

25 *Marsh v Arscott* (1982) 75 Cr App Rep 211; *Parkin v Norman* [1983] QB 92.
26 *Brutus v Cozens* [1973] AC 854.
27 *Jordan v Burgoyne* [1963] 2 QB 744.
28 *Atkin v DPP* (1989) 89 Cr App Rep 199.
29 Public Order Act 1986, s 4(2); *Atkin v DPP* (1989) 89 Cr App Rep 199; *R v Va Kum Hau* [1990] Crim LR 518.
30 *R v Horseferry Road Metropolitan Stipendary Magistrate, ex parte Siadatan* [1991] 1 QB 260.

'insulting' in s 4 of the Public Order Act apply equally to s 5. Disorderly behaviour is not defined and should be given its ordinary meaning. For the s 5 offence to be committed, it must be shown that there was a person present within the sight and hearing of the defendant at the time when the defendant was using threatening, insulting or abusive words or behaviour. It is not necessary for such a person to give evidence that they were harassed, alarmed or distressed. It is sufficient for a witness to give evidence that such a person was present and was likely to be caused harassment, alarm or distress. If a person is unlikely to be caused harassment, alarm or distress then no offence is committed. It was suggested that a police officer would be unlikely to be caused harassment, alarm or distress by threatening, abusive or insulting words, behaviour, writing, signs or other visible representations or by disorderly conduct. However, it has been confirmed that a police officer can be a person likely to be caused harassment, alarm or distress, and it is a question of fact whether an officer actually is so affected.[31]

The offence can be committed in a public or private place, but not inside a dwelling.[32] By s 6(4), a person is guilty of a s 5 offence only if he or she intends his or her words or behaviour or writing or other visible representation to be threatening, abusive or insulting or is aware that it may be threatening, abusive or insulting, or intends his or her behaviour to be, or is aware it may be, disorderly. The question of whether a person has the requisite intention under s 6(4) is answered subjectively. Proving intention or awareness on the part of the defendant that his or her words, behaviour or a visible representation might cause harassment, alarm or distress is insufficient. It by no means follows from this that the defendant intended or was aware that he or she may have been threatening, abusive or insulting.[33]

Under s 5(3), it is a defence to a charge under s 5 for the defendant to prove that:

(a) he or she had reason to believe that there was no person in hearing or sight who was likely to be caused harassment, alarm or distress; or
(b) he or she was inside a dwelling and had no reason to believe that the words or behaviour used or writing, sign or other visible representation displayed would be heard or seen by persons outside; or
(c) that his or her conduct was reasonable.

Reasonableness is judged by objective standards. It is for the defendant to prove on the balance of probabilities that his or her conduct was reasonable.[34] The s 5 offence is triable only summarily and it is punishable by a fine.

---

31 *DPP v Orum* [1988] 3 All ER 449.
32 Public Order Act 1986, s 5(2); *Chappell v DPP* (1989) 89 Cr App Rep 82.
33 *DPP v Clarke* (1992) 94 Cr App Rep 359.
34 Ibid.

PART III

MEETINGS OF COMPANIES INCORPORATED UNDER THE COMPANIES ACTS

CHAPTER 12

THE CONTROL AND MANAGEMENT OF COMPANIES

Introduction

Part III of this book deals with the various meetings that are held in connection with companies incorporated under the Companies Acts. The general principles governing meetings of all kinds are discussed in Part I and, in many places in that Part, reference is made to cases concerned with companies registered under the Companies Acts for illustration of those principles. This Part, however, is confined to a consideration of the meetings held in connection with such companies.

Division of powers

A company is recognised in law as being a distinct legal person.[1] However, being an artificial entity, it is only capable of acting through its duly constituted organs. These organs are the shareholders entitled to vote, acting in general meeting, and the board of directors. The Companies Act 1985[2] provides that certain corporate activities may only be done by one or other organ of the company. So far as the shareholders acting in general meeting are concerned, the Act provides that certain things may only be done by the meeting in a particular way. The Act lays down five particular ways in which the general meeting may engage in a corporate act. These are by special resolution, extraordinary resolution, ordinary resolution, elective resolution or written resolution. Special resolutions and extraordinary resolutions require, in order to be passed, a three-fourths majority of the votes cast at the meeting. An ordinary resolution requires a simple majority. Elective resolutions and written resolutions require unanimous agreement by all members entitled to attend and vote.

Those powers which are not required by the Act to be exercised by a particular organ are normally divided between the corporate organs by the company's articles of association. The provisions of the articles of association cannot, however, have the effect of relaxing the provisions of the Act. This

---

1 *Salomon v Salomon & Co* [1897] AC 22, HL.
2 This Act is referred to in this Part as the 'Act', and references in this Part to sections will, unless otherwise stated, be to sections of this Act.

means that where the Act requires certain things to be done in general meeting by special or extraordinary resolution, the articles may not provide for them to be done by a lesser majority in general meeting. On the other hand, anything which may be done by a simple majority can, under the articles of association, be required to be done by a greater majority.

The articles of association are one of the two constituent documents of the company. (The other is the memorandum of association.) The articles lay down the rules by which the company will conduct its affairs. They may only be altered by special resolution,[3] and then only within the parameters laid down by the mandatory provisions of the Act. A company limited by shares, which is the most common form of company, may adopt Table A of the Companies (Tables A–F) Regulations 1985, or it may adopt Table A with some amendments. If a company lodges no articles of association of its own at the time of its registration then Table A will become that company's articles.[4] The provisions of Table A have been referred to as examples of company rules in Part I and will also be referred to in this context in this Part.

Unless the Act or the articles otherwise provide, a company can authorise any act by an ordinary resolution, that is, one passed at a general meeting by a bare majority of votes.

> 'Unless some provision to the contrary is to be found in the charter or other instrument by which the company is incorporated, the resolution of a majority of the shareholders, duly convened, upon any question with which the company is legally competent to deal, is binding upon the minority, and consequently upon the company, and every shareholder has a perfect right to vote upon any such question, although he may have a personal interest in the subject-matter opposed to, or different from, the general or particular interests of the company.'[5]

This is, however, limited to matters which the company is legally entitled to transact. If all the shareholders agree to a corporate act which is illegal or unlawful, this is ineffective and the company does not thereby acquire the power necessary for that purpose. It is also the case that if the articles or the Act have removed control of certain matters from the general meeting, then the majority of shareholders will not have any power in relation to those matters. Where the articles (rather than the Act) have deprived the general meeting of power, however, it is always open to the company to alter the articles by special resolution.

Most company articles provide that the business of the company shall be managed by the directors. Where the articles provide to this effect, then the power of the shareholders in general meeting to interfere with the running of

---

3 Companies Act 1985, s 9.
4 Ibid, s 8(2).
5 *North-West Transportation Co v Beatty* (1887) 12 App Cas 589, 593. But for a very different approach to personal interests, see *Clemens v Clemens Bros Ltd* [1976] 2 All ER 268.

the company is very limited. Nevertheless, there are circumstances where, notwithstanding the fact that the power to manage the business of the company resides with the directors, the general meeting may exercise the management power. This power will transfer to the general meeting if the directors waive their power, are unable to exercise it because of conflicting personal interests, are deadlocked or are inquorate. In these circumstances, the general meeting may act by ordinary resolution.[6]

The provision of Table A which confers on the directors the power to manage the company's business is reg 70. This regulation provides as follows:

'Subject to the provisions of the Act, the memorandum and the articles and to any directions given by special resolution, the business of the company shall be managed by the directors who may exercise all the powers of the company. No alteration of the memorandum or articles and no such direction shall invalidate any prior act of the directors which would have been valid if that alteration had not been made or that direction had not been given. The powers given by this regulation shall not be limited to any special power given to the directors by the articles and a meeting of directors at which a quorum is present may exercise all powers exercisable by the directors.'

If the members of a company disapprove of the action of its directors on a matter which is within the powers of the directors, they cannot, by passing a resolution, annul the directors' decision. The members can remove the directors by ordinary resolution (see Chapter 17) or, by special resolution, control the directors for the future by altering the articles. Where the company has an article in the form of reg 70, then the general meeting may also control the directors for the future by giving directions by special resolution; however, such directions cannot invalidate an act which has already been carried out by the directors.

Ultra vires acts

If a company acts outside the powers conferred on it by its memorandum of association, this no longer renders the relevant act invalid.[7] However, a shareholder may bring proceedings to restrain an act outside the powers conferred on the company in the memorandum, although these proceedings cannot be brought where the act to be done is 'in fulfilment of a legal obligation arising from a previous act of the company'.[8] It should, however, be noted that the directors are liable for breach of duty if they are responsible for the company acting outside the powers laid down in its memorandum. They may only escape liability for this breach of duty if the general meeting passes a

---

6 *Barron v Potter* [1914] 1 Ch 895; *Foster v Foster* [1916] 1 Ch 532.
7 Companies Act 1985, s 35(1).
8 Ibid, s 35(2).

special resolution specifically relieving them from their breach. A special resolution which merely ratifies the corporate act is insufficient to save the directors from the consequences of their breach of duty.[9]

Where the directors act outside the range of powers allocated to them by the Act and the articles of association by, for example, usurping powers which belong to the general meeting, then the act of the directors will still be valid in favour of a person dealing with the company in good faith.[10] Members have the right to bring proceedings to restrain the doing of an act which is beyond the power of the directors, but this right is subject to the same limitations, as discussed above, as the right to restrain the doing of an act which is outside the capacity of the company as laid down in its memorandum.[11] Where the directors act outside the powers allocated to them then they are liable for a breach of duty to the company.[12] It seems likely that an ordinary resolution of the company is sufficient to excuse the directors from this breach of duty, although directors wishing to ensure their position beyond doubt in such circumstances would be advised to seek the passing of a special resolution excusing them from liability.

Commencement of litigation

It seems that where companies have an article in the form of reg 70 then the power to initiate litigation belongs to the board of directors.[13] The case of *John Shaw & Sons (Salford) Ltd v Shaw*[14] makes it clear that, where the board of directors has been delegated general powers of management, the general meeting is incapable of discontinuing litigation initiated by the board. Possibly, however, where the company has an article in the form of reg 70, the general meeting may be able to direct the board of directors by special resolution to discontinue litigation. Where the directors' decision not to commence litigation is in breach of their duties to the company then it seems that the general meeting has the right to initiate the relevant litigation.[15] It is also the case that the general meeting has the right to commence proceedings in the name of the company against the directors for breach of their duty.[16]

The circumstances in which a minority of shareholders can bring an action in the name of the company are very limited. They may do so, using the form of action known as the derivative action, where there is a fraud on the

---

9 Companies Act 1985, s 35(3).
10 Ibid, s 35A(1).
11 Ibid, s 35A(4).
12 Ibid, s 35A(5).
13 Compare the approaches in *Marshall's Valve Gear Co Ltd v Manning, Wardle & Co Ltd* [1909] 1 Ch 267 and *John Shaw & Sons (Salford) Ltd v Shaw* [1935] 2 KB 113, HL.
14 [1935] 2 KB 113, HL.
15 *Re Argentum* [1975] 1 All ER 608, which explains *Marshall's Valve Gear Co Ltd v Manning, Wardle & Co Ltd, supra,* on this basis.
16 *Pender v Lushington* (1877) 6 ChD 70.

minority.[17] A minority shareholder is not, however, permitted to bring an action in its own name for a wrong done to the company. This would breach the rule in *Foss v Harbottle*, which stipulates that the proper plaintiff for a wrong done to the company is the company itself.[18] Minority shareholders may, nevertheless, petition the court under s 459 of the Act on the basis that the affairs of the company are being conducted in a manner which is unfairly prejudicial to company members.

---

17 See, for example, *Burland v Earle* [1902] AC 83; *Menier v Hooper's Telegraph Co* (1874) LR 9 Ch App 350; *Pavlides v Jensen* [1956] Ch 565; *Prudential Assurance Co Ltd v Newman Industries Ltd (No 2)* [1982] 2 WLR 31.

18 (1843) 2 Hare 461.

CHAPTER 13

MEETINGS OF MEMBERS (INCLUDING CLASSES OF MEMBERS AND OF DEBENTURE HOLDERS)

Annual general meetings

Subject to the elective regime under s 366A of the Act, which is discussed below, every company is in each year required to hold a general meeting as its annual general meeting. This is provided for in s 366(1), where it is further provided that the annual general meeting must be in addition to any other meetings in the year and shall be specified as the annual general meeting in the notices calling it. Section 366(3) provides that not more than 15 months shall elapse between the date of one annual general meeting of the company and that of the next. However, a relaxation is made by s 366(2) so that as long as a company holds its first annual general meeting within 18 months of its incorporation, it need not hold it in the year of its incorporation nor in the following year. Failure to comply with these provisions on the holding of meetings will, according to s 366(4), render the company and each of its officers in default liable to a fine.

The elective regime for private companies, which was introduced into the 1985 legislation, allows private companies to dispense with the holding of annual general meetings.[1] The provisions of s 366A, which allow private companies to escape the requirements in s 366, require a private company to pass an elective resolution in order to dispense with the holding of annual general meetings. The requirements for the passing of an elective resolution are laid down in s 379A. These requirements are discussed in Chapter 17.

Leaving aside the case of a private company which has elected to dispense with annual general meetings under s 366A, if an annual general meeting is not held in compliance with s 366 the Secretary of State may, on the application of a member, direct the calling of a general meeting.[2] Such a meeting is, subject to any directions given by the Secretary of State, to be regarded as an annual general meeting. If, through default in holding a meeting in one year, the Secretary of State orders a meeting to be held and it is so held in the following

---

1 For the definition of 'private company', see s 1(3).
2 Section 367(1).

year, the meeting is not to be treated as the annual general meeting for the year in which it is held unless at that meeting it is so resolved.[3] Default in complying with any directions given by the Secretary of State with respect to the holding of meetings renders the company and every officer in default liable to a fine.[4]

The articles may specify what is to be usual business at an annual general meeting. However, Table A of the Companies (Tables A–F) Regulations 1985, unlike its predecessor in the 1948 legislation, contains no such provision. Where, as in the present Table A, there is no such provision then it is likely that all business must be treated as special business. The consequence of this is that no business may be transacted without previous notice of its general nature being given to members.[5] In order to avoid the inconvenience of this, it is suggested that companies incorporate into their articles of association a provision in the form of reg 52 of Table A of the Companies Act 1948. This regulation provides that all business transacted at an annual general meeting or an extraordinary general meeting is deemed to be special, with the exception of declaring a dividend, the consideration of the accounts and balance sheets, the consideration of the reports of the directors and auditors, the election of directors in the place of those retiring, and the appointment of, and fixing of the remuneration of, the auditors.

The appointment of auditors is a matter with which every company is required to deal at each general meeting before which accounts are laid. The auditor or auditors so appointed then hold office until the conclusion of the next such meeting.[6] The provisions on the appointment of auditors are part of a code designed to buttress the independence of auditors and are considered in more detail in Chapter 18.

In addition to those matters required by the articles of association and the Act to be dealt with at annual general meetings, s 376(6) provides that the business of an annual general meeting includes resolutions proposed by members under s 376. This section permits members holding one-twentieth or more of the total voting rights or at least 100 members of the company, holding shares paid up to an average sum of at least £100, to require the company, at the expense of the requisitioning members, to give all members notice of resolutions proposed to be moved and also to circulate to members a statement in support of that resolution of not more than 1000 words.

In the absence of fraud, the directors have a right to select the place of meetings.[7] The power of the directors to select the place of meetings is a fiduciary power which must be exercised in the interests of the company. If it were called at a place or time which would be inconvenient for shareholders so

---

3 Section 367(4).
4 Section 367(3).
5 *R v Hill* (1825) 4 B&C 444.
6 Section 385(2).
7 *Martin v Walker* (1918) 145 LTN 377.

as to have the effect of restricting the attendance, this would be a wrongful exercise of their power, and could be challenged.[8]

During the whole of the annual general meeting the register of the interests of directors of the company in shares or debentures of the company and related companies required to be kept by s 325 of the Act is by reg 29 of Sch 13, Part IV of the Act required to be open to the inspection of the members. It must also be produced at the commencement of the meeting.

Extraordinary general meetings

General meetings of the shareholders, other than annual general meetings, are called extraordinary general meetings (reg 36 of Table A). These meetings are held for the transaction of business which cannot wait until the next annual general meeting.[9] They will usually be convened by the directors when they think proper (reg 37). They may also be called by any member or any director if there are too few directors in the UK to call a meeting (reg 37).

Under s 368, which expressly overrides any contrary provision in the articles, the directors must call a meeting on the requisition of members holding not less than one-tenth of such of the paid up capital as carries the right of voting at general meetings (or if the company has no share capital, of members representing not less than one-tenth of the voting rights of all members having the right to vote at general meetings). The requisition must state the objects of the meeting, and it must be signed by the requisitionists and deposited at the company's registered office. For this purpose, it is generally accepted in practice that a requisition sent through the post is due compliance with the requirement to deposit. The requisition may consist of several documents, each signed by one or more requisitionist (s 368(3)). Where several documents are used for the requisition, they must be in like form. This requirement does not mean they must be in exactly the same form.[10] Where a requisition is made by holders of shares held jointly, such requisition must be signed by all the joint holders.[11]

Section 368(4) provides that if the directors do not proceed within 21 days to convene a meeting to be held within 28 days from the date of the notice convening the meeting, then those representing at least half the total voting rights of the requisitionists may proceed themselves to convene a meeting (s 368(4) and (8)). The requirement that the directors must convene the meeting for a date within 28 days from the date of the notice convening the meeting (which must be given within 21 days from the date of the deposit of the requisition) was only added in the Companies Act 1989. There is a curious

---

8 *Cannon v Trask* (1875) LR 20 Eq 669.
9 The directors of a public company the net assets of which fall to one half or less of its called-up share capital must call an extraordinary general meeting: s 143.
10 *Fruit and Vegetable Growers' Association v Kekewich* [1912] 2 Ch 52.
11 *Patent Wood Keg Syndicate v Pearse* (1906) WN 164.

mismatch between this provision and reg 37 of Table A which requires the directors to convene a meeting pursuant to a requisition within eight weeks of the date of the receipt of the requisition. It is the case, nevertheless, that the provisions of the Act should be taken to prevail.

A meeting convened by the requisitionists as a result of the directors' failure duly to proceed to convene a meeting may not be held after the expiration of three months from the date of the deposit of the requisition. When requisitioning a meeting, the requisitionists must do so in the same manner, as nearly as possible, as that in which meetings are convened by the directors (s 368(5)). The company must pay the reasonable expenses of requisitionists incurred as a result of convening a meeting, but may deduct the same amount from remuneration falling due to the defaulting directors (s 368(6)). The requisitionists are also entitled to convene a meeting where the directors convene a meeting to deal with part only of the business specified in the requisition. In this case the requisitionists may convene a meeting only for the purpose of considering the business omitted from the notice sent out by the directors.[12] Presumably, in order to convene such a meeting to deal with the business omitted from the notice sent out by the directors, those representing at least half of the total voting rights of the requisitionists must be involved in the convening of the meeting. Finally, it should be noted that any director of the company or any voting member of the company is entitled to apply to the court under s 371 for an order requiring the holding of a meeting. Where the court makes such an order the meeting must be held and conducted in the manner which the court thinks fit.

The only person other than the directors or members entitled to require the holding of an extraordinary general meeting is a resigning auditor. Pursuant to s 392A, where an auditor's notice of resignation is accompanied by a statement of circumstances which, in the auditor's opinion, should be brought to the attention of members or company creditors, then the auditor may requisition the directors to convene an extraordinary general meeting. The purpose of holding such a meeting will be to allow the meeting to receive information about and consider the circumstances which have given rise to the auditor's concern (s 392A(2)). The auditor may request the company to circulate to its members a statement in writing concerning the circumstances connected with his or her resignation. Such a statement should be circulated before the relevant meeting (s 392A(3)). The directors must convene a meeting within 21 days, to be held before the end of 28 days from the date of the notice convening the meeting. Any director who fails to take reasonable steps to secure the convening of such a meeting is guilty of an offence (s 392A(5)). Unless the auditor's statement to the members is received too late, the notice convening the meeting should indicate that such a statement has been made and a copy should be sent to every member of the company who is entitled to receive notices convening meetings (s 392A(4)). If, for any

---

12 *Isle of Wight Railway Co v Tahourdin* (1883) 25 ChD 320.

reason, every member of the company does not receive a copy of the resigning auditor's notice then the auditor is entitled to require the statement to be read out at the meeting (s 392A(6)). The right of a resigning auditor to have the contents of their statement made known to the members is subject to the ability of the company or any aggrieved person to apply to the court on the basis that the rights are 'being abused to secure needless publicity for defamatory matter'. Where such an application is made the court may order the auditor to pay the company's costs in part or in full (s 392A(7)). The provisions concerning resigning auditors are part of a more general series of provisions which are designed to strengthen the position of the company auditor. These provisions are further considered in Chapter 18.

Class meetings

(1) Under the Companies Act 1985

The capital of a company may be divided into classes of shares with different rights, whether as to dividend, capital or voting. Different classes may be created by the memorandum, the articles, the terms of issue of shares or by the terms of the resolution authorising the issue. The articles will often provide the conditions which must be fulfilled for the valid alteration of the rights attached to a class. It should, however, be noted that the standard set of articles contained in Table A contains no such provision. Rather, a complete code on the variation of class rights is contained in Chapter II of Part V of the Companies Act. Section 125 is the central provision of this code. It makes provision for the following four situations:

(a) *Where there are class rights, however conferred, and the articles make provision for the variation of those rights provided that the variation is not concerned with authority for allotment under s 80 or a reduction of share capital under s 135.* In this case, s 125(4) provides that, as long as the provision in the articles with respect to variation was included at the time of the company's original incorporation, the rights may only be varied in accordance with the provisions in the article.

(b) *Where there are class rights, however conferred, and the memorandum or articles make provision for the variation of those rights and the proposed variation is in relation to an authority for allotment under s 80 or a reduction of share capital under s 135.* In this situation, s 125(3) provides that the class rights may only be varied if either the holders of 75 per cent in nominal value of the issued shares of that class consent in writing or the variation is sanctioned by an extraordinary resolution at a meeting of the holders of that class of shares. If the memorandum or articles provide further requirements for variation in this context then compliance with those requirements is also necessary.

(c) *Where the class rights are conferred in the memorandum and neither the memorandum nor the articles make provisions with respect to variation of those rights.* In this situation, s 125(5) provides that the class rights may only be varied if all members of the company agree to the variation.

(d) *Where the class rights are attached otherwise than by the memorandum and the articles make no provision with respect to variation of those rights.* In this situation, s 125(2) provides that the class rights may only be varied if either the holders of 75 per cent in nominal value of the issued shares of that class consent in writing, or an extraordinary resolution is passed at a class meeting of the holders of that class. If there is any other requirement for variation in this situation, however imposed, compliance with this must also take place.

For the purposes of the application of s 125, it should be noted that an alteration of a provision in the articles for variation of class rights is itself a variation of those rights (s 125(7)) and an abrogation of class rights is also to be treated as a variation (s 125(8)).

Where the above rules as to variation of class rights require the holding of a meeting, then s 125(6) makes the requirements of s 369 as to the length of notice for calling company meetings, the requirements of s 370 as to meetings and votes, and the requirements of ss 376 and 377 as to circulation of members' resolutions, as well as any provisions in the articles relating to general meetings, so far as applicable, relevant. This is subject to two conditions: first, at any meeting other than an adjourned meeting, the quorum is two persons holding at least one-third of the nominal value of the issued shares of the relevant class (at an adjourned meeting the quorum is one person holding shares of the relevant class); and, secondly, any holders of shares in the relevant class may demand a poll. However, it should be noted that where the articles make detailed provisions as to the conduct of class meetings, these probably override the provisions of s 125(6). This is a vexed point and it may be wise to ensure that the two qualifications regarding quorum and a poll are complied with in any case. (The provisions of s 369 on notice for calling company meetings including notice for members' resolutions and s 370 on meetings and votes are discussed in Chapters 14 and 16 respectively.)

(2) On the directions of the court pursuant to s 425

The meetings referred to above are convened by the company in the same way as meetings of the company are convened, but there is another kind of class meeting which may be held. This is under s 425. Under this section, where a compromise or arrangement is proposed between a company and its creditors or any class of them or between the company and its members or any class of them, the court may, on the application of the company or of any creditor or member of the company, or, in the case of a company being wound up or subject to an administration order, of the liquidator or the administrator, order a meeting of the creditors or class of creditors, or of the members of the company or class of members, as the case may be, to be summoned in such manner as the court directs. If a majority in number representing three-fourths in value of the creditors or class of creditors or members or class of members, as the case may be, present and voting either in person or by proxy at the meeting, agree to any compromise or arrangement, the compromise or arrangement, if sanctioned by the court, becomes binding on all the creditors or the class of creditors, or on the members or class of members, as the case may be, and also on the company or, in the case of a company in the course of being wound up, on the liquidator and contributories of the company. (The expression 'arrangement' includes a reorganisation of the share capital of the company by the consolidation of shares of different classes or by the division of shares into shares of different classes or by both those methods (s 425(6)(b)).) A 'compromise or arrangement' may include a complete change in the company's capital structure, and may even amount to its acquisition by another company.[13] In the latter case, however, the court will impose a heavy burden on those who support the scheme to show that it is a fair one.[14]

Pursuant to s 426, a company proposing a scheme of arrangement under s 425 is required to give certain specified information regarding the effect of the scheme and the interests of directors and debenture stock trustees. This information must be contained in a statement which must accompany every notice summoning the required meeting under s 425. Failure to provide such a statement makes the company and every defaulting officer liable to a fine. Liquidators, administrators and trustees under a debenture trust deed are deemed to be officers for this purpose (s 426(6)). It should, however, be noted that mere compliance with the statutory requirement as to what must be disclosed in this statement may not be sufficient to ensure the court's sanction of the scheme. In particular, if there has been a subsequent change in the directors' material interests which is not disclosed to or before the relevant meeting the court will need to be satisfied that no reasonable person would have changed their mind and their vote in the light of that information before it will sanction the scheme of arrangement.[15]

Section 425 is a useful provision enabling all the members and creditors to be bound by a scheme of which the majorities of the various classes approve. Sometimes difficult questions as to what constitutes a separate class for the purposes of the section are raised. Generally speaking, if either:

(a) certain shares have different rights from other shares, and those rights are relevant for consideration of the scheme, or
(b) certain shares are treated differently under the scheme from others,

13 *Re National Bank Ltd* [1966] 1 WLR 819.
14 *Re Hellenic & General Trust Ltd* [1976] 1 WLR 123.
15 *Re Minster Assets plc* [1985] BCLC 200.

then separate classes exist for the purpose of the section. It was certainly once thought that a single type of share with similar rights and which was to be treated uniformly by the scheme constituted a single and indivisible class.[16] In *Re Hellenic & General Trust Ltd*,[17] however, a single shareholder with 53 per cent of the shares was the subsidiary of the bank which would, under the scheme, obtain all the new ordinary shares to be issued by the company (the old shares being cancelled in return for cash compensation). It was held that the subsidiary had an interest in the 'purchaser's camp' distinct from the interest of the other shareholders. Consequently, the subsidiary formed a separate class, so that separate class meetings should have been held to approve the scheme. It is generally thought that the decision somewhat strains the meaning of 'class rights' and it seems that this notion of class rights should be confined strictly to the rules on schemes of arrangement under s 425. The case is unlikely to be treated as good authority in respect of any more general definition of class rights.

The meetings for the purpose of consenting to a scheme of arrangement are summoned by the order of the court and in accordance with its directions. Failure to comply with the court's directions may result in the court refusing to sanction the scheme.[18] Proxies may be used in meetings under s 425, provided the company is not in liquidation.[19] The form of a proxy for these purposes will be settled in chambers. Directors who hold proxies for or against a scheme must use them.[20]

The class meetings themselves do not constitute general meetings of the company. If the scheme requires either the consent of the company in general meeting, or some corporate act which has to be performed in general meeting, such as an increase or reduction of capital, then an extraordinary general meeting must be convened for this purpose. Such a meeting is convened by the directors in the ordinary way, and is not called on the direction of the court. Proxies for such general meeting must follow the form required by the articles. On proxies, see Chapter 16.

(3) In relation to compensation to directors for loss of office

As to class meetings that may be required to be held in connection with compensation to directors for loss of office, see Chapter 14.

---

16 *Re Alabama, New Orleans, Texas & Pacific Junction Railway* [1891] 1 Ch 213. 'Classes' of creditors may be a more flexible concept. For example, holders of matured insurance policies constitute a class separate from other policy-holders; *Sovereign Life Assurance Co v Dodd* [1892] 2 QB 573.

17 [1976] 1 WLR 123.

18 Cf *Re Anglo-Spanish Tartar Refineries* [1924] WN 222.

19 *Re Magadi Soda Co* [1925] WN 50.

20 *Re Dorman, Long & Co* [1934] Ch 635.

Meetings of debenture stockholders

Akin to class meetings are meetings of debenture stockholders. These will be convened and conducted in accordance with the provisions contained in the debenture stock trust deed. Under trust deeds made some years ago, the provisions for calling meetings of debenture stockholders are often inadequate for modern requirements. The quorum requirements are often so high that in practice they are difficult to attain, and these requirements often extend through to a meeting adjourned from the original date, through lack of quorum, to a later date. A second defect is often the very restricted powers for amendment of the deed; frequently, they cannot be used to enable the substitution of a similar debenture stock of another company in place of that under the trust deed. Such substitution is often very desirable in the case of a take-over bid for the company concerned, or if the parent company in a group wishes to rationalise the financial structure and borrowing of the group.

If the provisions under the trust deed are inadequate, the company has to have recourse to a scheme under s 425.

Where a meeting of debenture holders is held, each holder may vote in his or her own interests, but if the holder has conflicting interests in a capacity as shareholder of the company, or as a creditor of a different class, he or she must not vote in favour of the other interest, or, if he or she does, his or her vote may be open to challenge.[21]

A person may be entitled to vote at a meeting of debenture holders if debentures have been allotted to him or her, his or her name is in the register of debenture holders, and he or she has the right to call for duly sealed debentures and is bound to accept them.[22]

Debentures are often issued on the terms that the rights of the holders may be varied with the consent of a certain proportion of the holders or with the consent of a resolution passed by a particular majority at a meeting of the holders. Any such variation must, to be valid, be strictly in accordance with the terms of the debentures. A power of this kind to vary rights will not justify abandoning rights and a power to compromise can only be exercised if there is some dispute to compromise,[23] or if there is some compromise (but not abandonment) of rights.[24] Where there is no power to compromise then, in order to achieve a compromise, it will be necessary to resort to s 425.

---

21 *Re New York Taxi Cab Co* [1913] 1 Ch 1.
22 *Dey v Rubber & Mercantile Corporation* [1923] 2 Ch 528.
23 *Mercantile Investment Co v International Co of Mexico* [1893] 1 Ch 484n.
24 *Re N F U Development Trust Ltd* [1972] 1 WLR 1548.

CHAPTER 14

NOTICE OF MEETINGS

Introduction

Where all the members of a company entitled to be present at a meeting agree on a particular course proposed then, provided the matter is within the power of the general meeting, this will constitute a valid corporate act. The law which permits this is known as the doctrine of informal corporate acts,[1] and it is now supplemented by provisions in ss 381A–381C on written resolutions of private companies. Both these matters are further considered in Chapter 17. In the absence, however, of an informal corporate act or a written resolution under the provisions of ss 381A–381C, the company will only be validly assembled so as to be able to transact business where a meeting is convened by a proper notice given in accordance with the provisions of the Act and the company's articles. Generally, the notice must be written, must state the time and place of the meeting, and the nature of the business to be transacted except where such business is of a kind for which notice is not required under the articles. Consistent with the doctrine of informal corporate acts, however, any defect in notice will be cured if all the members entitled to be present at the meeting attend and agree on the course proposed.[2]

The general principles affecting notices of all classes of meetings are discussed fully in Chapter 2. The following remarks concern the particular law and practice governing meetings of shareholders.

Period of notice

The articles generally provide for a certain length of notice. Section 396(1), however, provides that any provision in the articles which allows for the calling of a meeting, except an adjourned meeting, on shorter notice than the period specified in that subsection, is void. The periods of notice specified are 21 days' notice in writing for an annual general meeting; or, in the case of a meeting which is not an annual general meeting or at which it is not proposed to pass a special resolution, seven days' notice in writing for an unlimited

1 *Parker & Cooper v Reading* [1926] 1 Ch 975; *Re Duomatic Ltd* [1969] 2 WLR 114; *Cane v Jones* [1980] 1 WLR 1451.
2 *Baroness Wenlock v River Dee Co* (1883) 36 ChD 681n.

company or 14 days' notice in writing for any other company. Where the articles are void as a result of contravening s 369(1), or are silent as to the period of notice, then these specified periods of notice will apply (s 369(2)). So far as the period of notice for a meeting at which a special resolution is to be proposed is concerned, s 378(2) provides for a period of 21 days' notice.

Periods of notice shorter than those stipulated in the Act or in the articles may be given in the following circumstances. In the case of an annual general meeting, short notice may be given if agreed to by all the members entitled to attend and vote (s 369(3)). In any other case, short notice may be given if agreed to by a majority in number of such members having between them 95 per cent in nominal value of the total voting rights at the meeting (ss 369(3) and (4), and 378(3)). It should, however, be noted that as a result of the introduction of the elective regime for private companies in the Companies Act 1989, a private company may elect to allow short notice with the consent of at least 90 per cent in nominal value of the total voting rights at the meeting (ss 369(4) and 378(3)). Such an election will only be effective if passed in accordance with the regime for elective resolutions in s 379A. This regime is considered in Chapter 17.

The number of days' notice must be clear.[3] This means that in calculating whether the period of notice has been given, the day upon which the notice is given or is deemed to be given and the day upon which the meeting is to be held must be excluded. Table A, reg 115 provides that notices are deemed to have been given 48 hours after they have been posted. Reliance on this provision, however, during a postal strike may be a ground for the grant of an injunction to a shareholder, who did not receive the notice in good time, to restrain the holding of the meeting.[4]

The proper authority for the issue of notices

It is usually the directors who are responsible for convening the annual general meeting and empowered to convene extraordinary meetings (see, for example, Table A, reg 37). This power to convene meetings is a power of the board, not of only some of the directors[5] (unless acting as a duly appointed committee with power to convene meetings).

A notice issued by the secretary without the authority of a resolution of the directors duly assembled at a board meeting is invalid,[6] and where a meeting is requisitioned under s 368 the secretary cannot validly summon a meeting without the authority of the board of directors.[7] A notice issued without such

---

3 *Mercantile Co v International Co of Mexico* [1893] 1 Ch 484n; *Re Hector Whaling Co* [1936] Ch 208; and see, for example, Table A, reg 38.

4 *Bradman v Trinity Estates plc* [1989] BCLC 757.

5 *Browne v La Trinidad* (1887) 37 ChD 1, 17.

6 *Re Haycroft Gold Reduction Co* [1900] 2 Ch 230.

7 *Re State of Wyoming Syndicate* [1901] 2 Ch 431; and see also s 368.

authority, either because no instructions have been given by the board for its issue or because the instructions were given by an improperly constituted board, may become a good notice if adopted and ratified by a proper board meeting held prior to the general meeting. As was said in *Hooper v Kerr* 'The question is whether, although the notice was not authorised beforehand, it has been so ratified now as to make it a good and valid notice ... The principle of the cases ... is that the ratification of an act purporting to be done by an agent on your behalf dates back to the performance of the act.'[8] In this context, note should also be taken of Table A, reg 92, which provides that all acts done by any meeting of directors, a committee of directors or by any person acting as a director shall, notwithstanding that it be afterwards discovered that there was some defect in the appointment of any such director or that they or any of them were disqualified, had vacated office, or were otherwise not entitled to vote, be valid as if every such person had been duly appointed, was qualified to be a director and entitled to vote. An article in this form may validate a meeting held on notices sent out by an irregularly constituted board.[9] As to the extent to which such an article will be effective, see *Morris v Kanssen.*[10]

Notices should be signed by the secretary, qualified by the words 'By Order of the Board', and the secretary should see that the board meeting, which has authorised the convening of a general meeting, was itself properly convened and that a quorum of directors was present. Where, however, the articles make no provision for the calling of meetings, two or more members holding not less than one-tenth of the issued share capital, or if the company does not have a share capital, not less than five per cent in number of the members of the company, may call a meeting (s 370(3)).

As to the powers of members to give notice of a meeting in certain circumstances, see Chapter 13.

To whom notices should be sent

(a) *Members.* Subject to any limitations in the articles, all members on the register are entitled to receive notice of meetings,[11] and if notice is not sent to any person entitled to receive it, the meeting is irregular and its proceedings invalid.[12] Articles normally provide that accidental failure to give notice will not invalidate a meeting or the proceedings.[13] However, if the failure to send a notice is deliberate, for example where the company

---

8 (1900) 83 LT 730.

9 *Transport Ltd v Schomburg* (1905) 21 TLR 305.

10 [1946] AC 459.

11 Section 370(2) and Table A, reg 38.

12 *Smyth v Darley* (1849) 2 HLC 789. Note also that in *Re A Company (No 00789 of 1987), ex parte Shooter* [1990] BCLC 384, it was held that the holding of an extraordinary general meeting without adequate notice, at which new shares were created, was grounds for a petition alleging unfairly prejudicial conduct under s 459.

13 *Re West Canadian Collieries* [1962] Ch 370; Table A, reg 39.

believes that notice to the address in a register will not reach the member and accordingly does not send one to that member, the saving of the article will not operate as the failure to send the notice is not accidental.[14]

(b) *Special classes of members.* Articles often prescribe that certain classes of members shall not be entitled to receive notice. An example of such a class are the holders of preference shares in cases where the preference shares do not confer the right to vote. If the preference shares do not confer the right to vote, but the articles make no special provision on notice, it is unclear whether the preference shareholders will be entitled to notice.[15] To exclude all doubt, articles which provide that certain classes of members are not to have a vote also often provide that they shall not be entitled to receive notices of or to attend meetings.

(c) *Joint holders of shares.* All joint holders must be given notice individually unless the articles, as they almost invariably do, provide that this shall not be necessary. Regulation 112 of Table A, for example, provides that notice to all joint holders may be given to the first-named joint holder in the register.

(d) *Persons entitled to a share as a result of the death or bankruptcy of a member.* In the absence of any provision in the articles, persons who become entitled to a share as a result of the death or bankruptcy of a member are not automatically entitled to notice of meetings, because they are not members of the company. It is common, however, for articles to provide, as does reg 38 of Table A, that notice be given to a person entitled to a share as a result of the death or bankruptcy of a member. It is unclear what such people should do with this notice since reg 31 of Table A provides that, before being registered as the holder of a share, a person entitled to a share as a result of death or bankruptcy is not entitled to attend or vote at any meeting of the company. To avoid this peculiar result, companies may well choose to diverge from the provisions of Table A and provide that notice need not be given to persons entitled to a share as a result of death or bankruptcy.

It should be noted in this context that a member who becomes bankrupt remains a member and is able to exercise the votes attached to his or her shares, notwithstanding that by taking appropriate steps under the appropriate provisions the trustee in bankruptcy might be able to secure registration as the holder of the shares.[16] A company cannot, therefore, treat a member who is known to be bankrupt in any other manner than they treat other members, whether in connection with sending notices to that member or accepting the votes of that member.

---

14 *Musselwite v C H Musselwite* [1962] Ch 964.
15 *Re Mackenzie* [1916] 2 Ch 450; *In re Warden & Hotchkiss* [1945] Ch 270, 278, but see s 370(2).
16 *Morgan & Gray* [1953] Ch 83.

(*e*) *Directors.* Articles commonly require that notice of meetings be given to the directors. Regulation 38 of Table A is an example of such an article.

(*f*) *Auditors.* The auditor is entitled to attend any general meeting and to receive all notices and other communications relating to such a meeting (s 391(a) and (b)). The auditor is also entitled to be heard on any part of the business affecting him or her as auditor (s 390(1)(c)).

(*g*) *Debenture holders.* As a result of a special provision in s 5(8), notice of a special resolution to alter the objects clause of a company's memorandum must be given not only to members, but also to holders of any debentures secured by a floating charge issued or first issued before 1 December 1947 or debentures which form part of the same series as any debentures so issued. The subsection requires the same notice to be given to debenture holders as is given to members of the company. The provision does not confer on relevant debenture holders the right to attend the meeting, rather its purpose is to give them the right to object to the alteration.

Method of service

Articles usually provide for the method of serving notices on the members and compliance with any method prescribed in the articles is necessary. If, for example, the articles require notice through the post and notice is, in fact, given in a newspaper advertisement, such notice would be irregular, and vice versa. It should be noted, however, that if a meeting is irregularly convened, a person who attends and takes part may be unable subsequently to complain of the irregularity. For example, at an adjourned general meeting, notice of which adjournment was given by circulars sent to shareholders but not by advertisement as required by the deed of settlement, it was resolved to make a call. A shareholder who was present and voted at the adjourned meeting was not entitled to take advantage of the irregularity of the notice.[17]

Insofar as the articles do not make any provision for service of notices of meetings, every such notice must be served on every member of the company (not merely those entitled to vote) in the manner in which notices are required to be served by the Table A for the time being in force (s 370(2)). These provisions are now found in regs 111–116 of Table A. Regulation 111 provides that notice for a company meeting shall be in writing. Regulation 112 provides that notice may be given to a member personally, by post or by leaving it at the registered address of the member. Where the notices are to be given by post, then reg 115 provides that the notice is deemed to have been given at the expiration of 48 hours after the envelope was posted. The same regulation further provides that it shall be conclusive evidence that notice was given if it was proved that an envelope containing the notice was properly addressed, stamped and posted.

---

17 *Re British Sugar Refinery Co* [1857] 26 LJ Ch 369.

An important feature of the regulations on notice in Table A is the provision which entitles a member whose registered address is outside the UK to have notices given at a stipulated address within the UK. The regulation goes on to provide, however, that if such a member does not provide a UK address, he or she will have no entitlement to receive any notices from the company (reg 112). The equivalent regulation in Table A to the 1948 Act was the subject of *Parkstone Ltd v Gulf Guarantee Bank plc.*[18] In this case, a member with an address in Gibraltar had also given the company an address in the UK for the service of notices. The company, however, sent a notice to the address in Gibraltar. The court held that this was a valid notice under reg 131 of the 1948 Table A. It seems unlikely that a similar result would have been produced on these facts if the regulation in question had been in the form of reg 112 of the present Table A. This is because reg 112, unlike the old reg 131, 'entitles' members to have notices given to them at their stipulated UK address.

In *Re Warden & Hotchkiss Ltd,*[19] it was held that where the articles do not provide (as Table A does) that notice need not be given to members whose only address is outside the UK but do provide that a notice will be deemed to be delivered when the letter containing it would have been delivered in the ordinary course of post, then notice need not be given to members with registered addresses abroad. It seems, however, that this decision should now be regarded as applying only to companies whose articles are in exactly the same form as those in Table A to the 1862 Act. In other cases, a reference to the ordinary course of post should not be construed as including only post within the UK.[20]

Persons situated abroad who do not have the right to receive notices to company meetings are those persons who are enemies or who are situated in enemy territory. The right of such people to receive notices is suspended so long as they remain an enemy or in enemy territory, and meetings are properly convened though no notice has been served upon a person who, if not an enemy, would be entitled to notice.[21]

Time and place of meeting

The notice must state the time and place of the meeting. The fixing of these is usually left by the articles to the discretion of the directors (see, for example, reg 38 of Table A); however, they must be reasonably convenient for the shareholders.

Although the court will not usually interfere with the powers and duties of directors in their management of the internal affairs of a company, directors will be restrained from fixing a particular date for holding the annual general

---

18 [1990] TLR 477.
19 [1945] Ch 270.
20 *Parkstone Ltd v Gulf Guarantee Bank plc* [1990] TLR 477.
21 *Re Anglo-International Bank* [1943] Ch 233.

meeting of the company for the purpose of preventing sha
exercising their voting powers.[22]

The real nature of the business to be transacted

The vote of the majority at a general meeting, as it binds both dissentient and
absent shareholders, must be a vote given on proper information. This is
consistent with the general principle that matters must be fairly put before the
meeting and the meeting itself must be conducted in the fairest possible
manner.[23]

The notice of an annual general meeting is not required to specify any
business that is declared by the articles not to be special business. Subject to
this principle, the notice for any company meeting must give a fair, candid and
reasonable explanation of the business intended to be transacted.[24] The test,
which is admittedly an extremely imprecise one, is that the notice should be in
sufficient detail and of sufficient clarity for a member reading it to be able to
determine whether he or she should attend the meeting and if necessary ask
questions, or whether the member may without concern allow the meeting to
pass the resolution without his or her attendance or enquiry. This test will
certainly not be satisfied if the notice merely says that details or copies of
resolutions may be seen at the company's offices or that copies will be
forwarded on request.[25]

Giving facilities for obtaining information is not equivalent to giving the
information. It is sometimes found that, rather than attempt to summarise
proposals or changes, companies will set out in full the relevant provisions,
often by way of an appendix. This procedure does not seem to be a proper
course for directors to follow. Even though it may contain all the relevant
material, it will be in so indigestible a form as to be an unfair presentation. The
proper procedure is for the notice to summarise the proposals and, if these
involve changes from existing provisions, to summarise the differences.
Shareholders may then be offered the full details for inspection on request, but
they will at least know what they are seeking. Such a procedure is disliked by
directors, who feel cautious lest some provision may unwittingly be summarised incorrectly or overlooked, but the information is more likely to be presented clearly using this procedure.

Notice of an annual general meeting must specify the meeting as such
(s 366(1)), and when it is proposed to pass a special or extraordinary resolution at any meeting, the notice of the meeting must specify that the resolution
is to be passed as a special or extraordinary resolution, as the case may be

---

22 *Cannon v Trask* (1875) LR 20 Eq 669.
23 *Tiessen v Henderson* [1899] 1 Ch 861.
24 *Kaye v Croydon Tramways* [1898] 1 Ch 358.
25 *Normandy v Ind Coope & Co* [1908] 1 Ch 84.

(s 378). Since this intention must be specified in relation to 'the resolution', the text of the resolution or its entire substance must be set out in the notice. There is no point in adding to the notice words such as 'with such amendments and alterations as may be determined at the meeting', because no amendment may be made to any such proposed resolution. If the resolution as passed is different from that specified in the notice, notice of intention to propose the resolution actually passed will not have been given as required by s 378, and it will therefore not be a special or extraordinary resolution, even if passed by the required majority.[26] On the other hand, if the irregularity is a mere typographical error or other slip which would be obvious in the light of the proposal and the information given, the resolution may be passed in its proper form and will be effective; it is not necessary to reconvene the meeting. The courts have, on various occasions, acted on this principle when confirming reductions of capital.

An ordinary resolution need not be passed in the exact terms of the notice, and under all ordinary forms of articles there is no need to specify a proposed ordinary resolution.[27] It is sufficient to specify the nature of the business. In *Betts & Co v MacNaghten*[28] the notice stated that the meeting was for the purpose of considering the following resolution with such amendments and alterations as should be determined upon at that meeting, 'That A, B, and C be appointed directors'. The notice was taken as read at the meeting and A, B, C and two other persons were appointed directors. It was held that the notice sufficiently indicated the special business to be transacted, and that the particularity of the names did not put greater restriction upon the meeting than there would have been had the notice been in general terms; and accordingly all five were properly appointed. So, too, an amendment to an ordinary resolution which has been set out in the notice will not invalidate the resolution. But this will only apply if the amendment renders the resolution less, and not more, onerous to the company or its members, for example where the remuneration to be paid to directors is, under the amended resolution, less than that proposed in the notice.[29] The reason for this is that shareholders may have given proxies, or desisted from voting, because they were content with the stated proposal, but might have had a different attitude had the more onerous proposal been proposed originally.

---

26 *MacConnell v Prill & Co* [1916] 2 Ch 57. But the members may agree to waive their rights to notice in accordance with s 369(3) (extraordinary resolutions) or s 378(3) (special resolutions).

27 Unless it is one of which special notice is required under s 379. This is discussed further in Chapter 17.

28 [1910] 1 Ch 430.

29 *Torbuck v Westbury (Lord)* [1902] 2 Ch 871. The resolution in this case was a special resolution, and the section of the Companies Act 1862 relating to special resolutions differed from s 378.

An annual general meeting may transact special business if (and only if) the notice provides for it[30] and there is nothing in the articles confining special business to extraordinary meetings. In practice, many companies convene an annual general meeting to transact the ordinary business followed by an extraordinary general meeting, on the same day, to conduct special business. At whatever type of meeting it is to be transacted, the purport of the special business must be stated in the notice convening the meeting. The transaction of that special business will otherwise be invalid.[31] (However, the transaction at a meeting of some business outside the object specified in the notice will not make the whole meeting irregular.)[32]

Where the notice deals with two separate resolutions the failure of the one will not invalidate the other, even in cases where they are closely associated.[33] If it is intended that one proposal should take effect only if another does, they should either be put in a single resolution or made interdependent in their terms.

Adjourned meetings

When a meeting is adjourned, it is customary to fix the day and time for the adjourned meeting. Notice of an adjournment of a meeting, where it is adjourned to a fixed date, is not necessary, unless the articles otherwise provide, for it is merely a continuation of the original meeting and will be confined to business specified in the original notice.[34] Regulation 45 of Table A provides for fresh notice to be given if the adjournment is for 14 days or more. In this case, reg 45 of the Table A provides for seven clear days' notice specifying time and place of the meeting, and the general nature of the business to be transacted. Where the articles, unlike Table A, require notice but make no provision regarding the length of notice for an adjourned meeting then the same notice must be given as for the original meeting. If, therefore, the meeting is not the annual general meeting, and if no business remains which requires a special resolution, 14 clear days' notice will be required. If the meeting is the annual general meeting, or any remaining business includes a special resolution, 21 clear days' notice will be required.

An adjourned meeting may only transact business which was unfinished at the first meeting or which could have been transacted within the terms of the notice of that meeting. To transact other business, a separate meeting should be convened to be held immediately after the adjourned meeting.

---

30 *Graham v Van Diemen's Land Co* (1856) 26 LJ Ex 73.
31 *Lawes' Case* (1852) 1 De GM & G 421; *Kaye v Croydon Tramways Co* [1898] 1 Ch 358.
32 *Re British Sugar Refinery Co* (1857) 26 LJ Ch 369.
33 *Cleve v Financial Corporation* (1873) LR 16 Eq 363.
34 *Kerr v Wilkie* (1860) 1 LT 501.

Notice of proposal to pay compensation to directors

The Act contains important provisions as to disclosing proposals to pay compensation for loss of office to directors. Under s 312, a company may not make any payment to a director in compensation for loss of office or in consideration of or in connection with his or her retirement from office unless the particulars as to the proposed payment and the amount are disclosed to the members of the company and the proposal for payment is approved by the company. Therefore, when any such payment is proposed, a meeting of the company must be held and the notice must contain the particulars required by this section. Section 313 requires similar disclosure and approval by the company of any payment made to any director of compensation for loss of office or as consideration for, or in connection with, retirement from office when any such payment is proposed to be made in connection with the transfer of the whole or any part of the undertaking and property of the company. The section applies whether the proposed payment is by the company itself or some other person, for example a bidder for the shares. Section 314 deals with the situation when a similar payment is proposed to be made to a director in connection with transfers of shares in the company resulting from certain classes of offers to purchase the shares mentioned in the section, which include offers conditional on acceptance to a given extent. In such cases it is the duty of the director to see that the particulars and amount of the proposed payment are disclosed in the offer to purchase the shares. Section 315 provides that any such proposed payment must be approved by a meeting of the holders of all the shares to which the offer relates and of all the other shares of that class or those classes of shares. The provisions of the Act and the articles as to the holding of general meetings, apply to meetings to be held under s 315. The Secretary of State, on the application of any person concerned, may direct a modification to those usual rules for the purpose of a meeting under this section (s 315(2)). (The section itself modifies the usual rules as to the consequences of a lack of quorum (s 315(3)).)

The limitations of these sections should be noted. Section 312 deals only with compensation for loss of office as a director. It does not deal with the loss of any other position, and in particular it does not cover compensation which the company is already contractually bound to make, for example on termination of employment of its managing director.[35] Where, as will commonly be the case, the board has the power to appoint a managing director on such terms and with such remuneration as it may determine (Table A, reg 84), s 312 simply does not apply and the general meeting has no voice. Broadly the same considerations apply to the other sections.

---

35 *Taupo Totara Timber Co Ltd v Rowe* [1978] AC 537.

Resolution circulated on the requisition of members

In the ordinary case, the business specified in the notice will be that which the convenors of the meeting think ought to be transacted. However, s 376 provides for the giving of notice of resolutions and circulation of statements relating to business proposed to be transacted at the insistence of persons other than the convenors of the meeting. It permits persons other than the convenors of the meeting, at their own expense, to require the company:

(a) to give notice of a resolution which may properly be moved and is intended to be moved at the next annual general meeting; and
(b) to circulate any statement with respect to any matter to be dealt with at any forthcoming general meeting. The statement must not be more than 1000 words.

The meeting itself can decide that any such notice or statement shall not be at the expense of the requisitionists. Requisitionists are therefore well advised to include in their resolutions one which puts the expenses of the requisition on the company. As appears from the foregoing summary, the requisitionists can have notice of a resolution given only for an annual general meeting. They can, however, secure the circulation of a statement relating to any proposal which is to be considered at any general meeting, whether or not an annual general meeting.

The requisition may only be given by the holders of not less than one-twentieth of the total voting rights exercisable at the meeting to which the requisition relates or by not less than 100 members holding shares in the company on which there has been paid up an average sum, per member, of not less than £100 (s 376(2)). Subsections (3), (4) and (5) provide for the method of serving the notice or statement. Subsection (3) provides that the resolution and statement should be circulated to all members of the company entitled to have notice of the meeting in the manner permitted for service of notice of the meeting. Notice of a resolution must also be given to any other member of the company by giving notice of its general effect in the manner permitted for giving notice of meetings of the company (sub-s (4)). Finally, sub-s (5) provides that a copy of the resolution or statement, or the notice of the effect of the resolution (under sub-s (4)) should be given in the same manner and as far as practicable at the same time as the notice of the meeting. Where such notice is not given at the same time as the notice of the meeting, it should be served as soon as practicable thereafter.

Section 377 sets out the circumstances in which the company will not be obliged to circulate a resolution or a statement under s 376. These circumstances include the situation where the company or any other person who claims to be aggrieved by the terms of any such statement applies to the court and the court is satisfied that the rights conferred by the section are being abused to secure needless publicity for defamatory matter (s 377(3)).

Meeting ordered to be held by the court

If, for any reason, it is impracticable to call or to conduct a meeting of a company, the court may order one to be convened and held, and may give such directions as to the calling and conduct of the meeting as it thinks expedient (s 371). The directions may include a provision that one member present in person or by proxy shall constitute a meeting. The court may call a meeting notwithstanding the opposition of some members.[36] (However, it may not call a meeting where to do so would override class rights.)[37] The power under s 371 is useful if there is a dispute as to the identity of the duly constituted directors able to call a meeting. It has also recently been used to call meetings in circumstances involving a petition under s 459 that the affairs of the company have been conducted in an unfairly prejudicial manner.[38]

Annual general meetings may be ordered to be held by the Secretary of State for Trade and Industry, on the requisition of any member of the company, but experience shows that it is difficult to persuade the Secretary of State to act (s 376).

Authentication of notices

A notice must be properly authenticated. Section 41 provides that a document requiring authentication by a company may be signed by a director, secretary or other authorised officer of the company. Section 744 provides that a notice is a document for this purpose.

---

36 *Re El Sombrero Ltd* [1958] Ch 900.
37 *BML Group Ltd v Harman* (1994) *The Times*, April 8, CA.
38 *Re Sticky Fingers Restaurant Ltd* [1991] BCC 754; *Re Whitchurch Insurance Consultants Ltd* [1993] BCLC 1359.

CHAPTER 15

QUORUM AND APPOINTMENT OF CHAIRMAN

Quorum

(1) General rules

The articles generally make provision as to the number of members who constitute a quorum, that is, the number of members who are entitled to transact business of the meeting so as to bind all the members. If the articles do not lay down the number of members necessary to form a quorum at a meeting of the company, it is provided by s 370(4) that two members personally present shall be a quorum. There is an exception to this rule for single member companies incorporated under s 1(3A), which is laid down in s 370A. This section provides that for such a company, notwithstanding anything to the contrary in its articles, its quorum for meetings is one.

Only persons entitled to vote are counted in a quorum,[1] although the articles may provide that this includes persons holding a proxy for a voting member (see, for example, Table A, reg 40). If the articles so permit, a person present by proxy only may be counted towards the quorum. Usually, however, one member cannot constitute a quorum no matter how many proxies that person holds.[2] This rule is, of course, subject to an exception for single member companies, and is also subject to several other exceptions discussed below.

Articles normally state what is to happen if no quorum is present when the meeting is due to begin. An example is that found in reg 41 of Table A which provides that, if within half an hour no quorum is present, the meeting stands adjourned for one week exactly and is to be held at the same place, or at such other time and place as the directors may determine. Under reg 41, this also applies if at any time during the meeting a quorum ceases to be present. Some companies may regard this requirement for a meeting to remain quorate as inconvenient as it may permit a member who is unhappy with the progress of the meeting to bring it to a halt by walking out. Problems such as this may, to some extent, be dealt with under the principles of law preventing abuse of quorum provisions (discussed below). Nevertheless, some companies may

---

1 *Young v South African Syndicate* [1896] 2 Ch 268; Cf *Re Greymouth-Point Elizabeth Railway Co* [1904] 1 Ch 32.
2 *Re Sanitary Carbon Co* [1877] WN 223.

not wish to include this particular requirement of the present Table A in their articles. Ordinarily, the quorum for an adjourned meeting is the same as that for any other meeting (see, for example, Table A, reg 40).

A question can arise whether two joint holders, present personally or by proxy, can be counted for the purpose of a quorum, the question being due to the article normally found (see Table A, reg 55) which has the effect that the first-named in the register in respect of a holding may vote so as to exclude the votes of the other. On principle, however, the answer must be that both can be counted for a quorum as both are members and both are entitled to vote. The votes of the second-named would be excluded if the first-named were to vote all the jointly held shares, but the first-named is not bound to do that and will not necessarily do so.

For the purpose of a quorum, a corporation which is itself a member of a company and which has authorised some person to act as its representative at any meeting of the company, under the provisions of s 375 of the Act, is regarded as personally present, not as present by proxy.[3] Restrictions imposed upon a proxy do not apply to such a representative. A person present by his or her attorney is not present in person, nor, it seems, is an executor of a deceased member counted for the purpose of a quorum if the article requires the members to be personally present,[4] even if the executor is entitled to be on the register though not yet entered.

(2) One-person meetings

The general principle that one person cannot constitute the quorum for a meeting has already been noted. Some exceptions to this principle are, however, recognised. The obvious exception is for single member companies incorporated under s 1(3A) (s 370A). Additionally, it seems that a meeting of one person would be valid where there was only one voting shareholder in a company, even if some voting shares were temporarily disenfranchised by, for example, the death of the holder. Similarly, in *East v Bennett Bros*,[5] it was held that the assent of the only preference shareholder was equivalent to a resolution passed by a separate meeting of preference shareholders.

In the case of general meetings, there are, moreover, two statutory exceptions to the rule that one person cannot constitute a meeting. The first relates to the Secretary of State's power under s 367 to call a meeting where there has been default in complying with s 366 on the calling of annual general meetings. Section 367(2) provides that, in giving directions for the calling of such a meeting, the Secretary of State may direct that one member of the company present in person or by proxy 'shall be deemed to constitute a meeting'. The second relevant statutory provision is s 371, which deals with the power of the

3 *In re Kelantan Cocoa Nut Estates Ltd* [1920] WN 274.
4 *Re Bowling & Welby's Contract* [1895] 1 Ch 663.
5 [1911] 1 Ch 163.

court to order a meeting. Again, sub-s (2) of this section allows the court to direct that one member present in person or by proxy is 'deemed to constitute a meeting'. The fact that both s 367(2) and s 371(2) use the expression 'deemed' suggests statutory recognition of the fact that one person could not ordinarily constitute a meeting and, therefore, reinforces the general rule about one-person meetings.

(3) Special class quorums

In the case of class meetings held to resolve a proposed variation of class rights, s 125(6) requires a quorum of two persons holding or representing by proxy at least one-third in nominal value of the issued shares of the class in question. So high a quorum is not always easy to assemble, and if no quorum is obtained the meeting will be adjourned. The subsection provides that at an adjourned meeting the quorum is one person, either in person or by proxy, holding shares of the class in question.

(4) Abuse of quorum provisions

Where a minority shareholder refuses to attend a meeting and thus prevents the formation of a quorum, this will be a ground for the court ordering the holding of a meeting under s 371.[6] Presumably, the same consequence would follow in a situation where the articles require that the meeting remains quorate throughout, as in Table A, reg 40, and minority members persistently frustrate the transaction of business by leaving the meeting.

Chairman

(1) Appointment

In the absence of any provisions in the articles as to who is to be chairman of a meeting, any member elected by the members present may be a chairman (s 370(5)). However, the articles generally provide who is to take the chair at meetings. Regulation 42 of Table A, for example, provides for the chairman of the board of directors or, in the absence of that chairman, some other director nominated by the directors, to be the chairman of a company meeting. If neither of these are present within 15 minutes of the time fixed for holding the meeting, or if neither is willing to act, the directors are to elect one of themselves to be chairman of the meeting and if there is only one director present and willing to act, that director shall be the chairman. Regulation 43

---

6 *Re El Sombrero Ltd* [1958] Ch 900; *Re H & R Paul & Son Ltd* (1974) 118 SJ 166; *Re Opera Photographic Ltd* [1989] BCLC 763.

provides that if no director is willing, or none is present within 15 minutes, the members present may choose one of themselves to be the chairman.[7]

(2) Authority

The authority which a chairman has is usually delegated to him or her by the company under its articles or by that meeting by which he or she is appointed. Where a number of persons assemble and put a person in the chair they confer on that person by agreement the conduct of that assembled body. The person presiding over a general meeting of shareholders is, in the capacity as chairman of the meeting, acting as the representative of the members present at the meeting, not as the representative of the directors. The chairman's authority, which is acquired from the meeting, enables the chairman to do everything required to ascertain the opinion of the majority, to allow a proper discussion of the questions to be decided, and to ensure that the proceedings are conducted in accordance with the articles. The chairman must, of course, act fairly and allow all members who wish to speak to a motion to have a reasonable opportunity to do so, even if there is clearly a majority who have already made up their minds.

(3) Duties

It is the duty of the chairman to preserve order; to conduct the proceedings in a proper manner; and to take care that the sense of the meeting is properly ascertained with regard to any question which is properly before the meeting.[8] Thus, in the absence of express provisions in the articles, 'the details of the proceedings must be regulated by the persons present and by the chairman, and if his decision is quarrelled with it must be regulated by the majority of those present'.[9] But where the articles expressly provide for the conduct of meetings, the provisions contained therein must be followed.

(4) Powers

The powers of the chairman must be exercised impartially. It is the chairman's duty to conduct the meeting in such a way that the business thereof is facilitated and the results of that business clearly defined. It is the duty of a chairman to maintain his or her ruling on points of procedure. If the chairman's ruling is wrong, he or she may, of course, be called upon to answer for his or her conduct, and legal proceedings may follow, which may result in the proceedings of the meeting being declared invalid.[10] Generally, however, the

---

7 *Re Salcombe Hotel Development Corporation Ltd* (1989) 5 BCC 807. See also *Re Bradford Investments* [1991] BCLC 224, in which a proxy assumed the position of temporary chairman in order to elect a proper chairman.

8 *National Dwelling Society v Sykes* [1894] 3 Ch 159; *R v D'Oyly* (1840) 12 A&E 139.

9 *Wandsworth Gaslight Co v Wright* (1870) 22 LT 404.

10 *Henderson v Bank of Australasia* (1890) 45 ChD 330.

chairman of a general meeting has prima facie to decide all incidental questions which arise at such a meeting and require decision at that time.[11]

This general power of the chairman and its concomitant limitations have been summarised as follows:

'Where a chairman frustrates the business of a meeting by wilfully and without good reason preventing that business from being considered, the meeting may in view of his gross violation of duty supersede him as chairman and go on to transact the business. But if in good faith the chairman gives a decision upon a matter of difficulty, such as has arisen in connection with the notice in this case, I am not prepared to hold that his decision can be ignored and overturned there and then. In my opinion in such a case his decision must stand until it is set aside by the Court, or by a general meeting properly convened for that purpose.'[12]

More specifically, the chairman has the following powers:

(a) *To regulate the course of the proceedings at the meeting.* In the case of dispute the chairman is entitled to determine who should address the meeting, and protect the speaker from interruption. The chairman is also entitled to prevent discussion taking place which is not relevant to the business of the meeting.

The business transacted must come within the scope of the notice given, and the chairman should refuse to allow any proposed resolution to be put to the meeting which does not come within the scope of the notice. The chairman is bound, however, to allow the proposal of all legitimate and germane resolutions and amendments, and a refusal to do so will invalidate that part of the proceedings, because such refusal may amount to the withdrawal of a material and relevant question from the meeting. In *Henderson v Bank of Australasia*, Cotton LJ observed: '[T]he chairman was entirely wrong in refusing to put the amendment, and ... the resolutions which were passed cannot be allowed to stand, because the chairman, under a mistaken idea as to what the law was which ought to have regulated his conduct, prevented a material question from being brought before the meeting'.[13]

Amendments to resolutions must also come within the scope of the notice convening the meeting and conform to any provisions of the articles as to notice or other requirements. Much difficulty may arise from amendments. It seems to be the case that no amendment of any substance should be accepted to a special or extraordinary resolution (see Chapters 14 and 17). So far as an ordinary resolution is concerned, notice of an amendment is not necessary, at any rate so long as the amendment cuts

---

11 *Re Indian Zoedone Co* (1884) 26 ChD 70.
12 These words are believed to have been used by Lord Wark in *Melville v Graham-Yooll*, an unreported case referred to in [1936] SLT 54.
13 (1890) 45 ChD 330, 346.

down the effect of the resolution, notice of which was originally given, or if the notice stated that the resolution might be passed with such alterations as should be agreed upon.[14] No amendment radically altering the originally proposed resolution should be accepted. If there is the slightest doubt as to whether an amendment is in order or not, it should be allowed to be put. This will safeguard the ultimate resolution if it turns out in the end that the amendment is in fact relevant and germane to the resolution. The chairman often has to make up his or her mind at once upon the validity of amendments, and when the chairman is fairly certain that the amendment will be lost, there is no real harm done in allowing an amendment which may not be covered by the notice of the meeting. Thus, a chairman should not reject an amendment, if proposed, on the grounds that it has no chance of success. To do so would put the original resolution in danger of a technical objection, which may have no substance in fact.

Where the chairman does rule an amendment out of order, there is no obligation on the part of the mover of the amendment to contest that ruling or to leave the meeting. It is not necessary for the mover to keep up an altercation with the chairman, nor does the mover lose any right to later object by acting under the ruling of the chairman.[15]

Where notice has been given of several resolutions, each resolution must, if any member so requires, be put separately and not en bloc. The poll thereon must in any event be taken separately.[16] In this context, it should also be noted that at a meeting of a public company a motion for the appointment of two or more directors cannot be made by a single resolution unless that course is resolved upon by the meeting without dissent. If it is not so resolved, the appointment of each director must be resolved upon by a separate resolution (s 292).

(b) *To close the meeting with its consent.* When the views of the minority have been heard, it is competent for the chairman, with the sanction of a vote of the meeting, to declare the discussion closed and to put the question to vote.[17] This procedure can be important if a minority are wasting time and repeating arguments or digressing into irrelevancies.

(c) *To adjourn the meeting.* See Chapter 19.

(d) *To make arrangements for taking a poll and to receive or reject proxies.* The chairman's decision as to the rejection of proxies will be decisive until reversed by the court.

(e) *To give a casting vote.* The chairman has no casting vote unless it is so provided in the articles. Table A, reg 50 does so provide. A casting vote may be exercised only if there is an equality of valid votes. If the chairman

---

14 *Betts & Co v MacNaghten* [1910] 1 Ch 430.
15 *Henderson v Bank of Australasia* (1890) 45 ChD 330.
16 *Blair Open Hearth Furnace Co v Reigart* (1913) 108 LT 665.
17 *Wall v London & Northern Assets Corporation* [1898] 2 Ch 469.

does not exercise his or her casting vote in such a situation, the motion is not carried. A chairman may also have an ordinary vote if he or she is a member of the company (as is usually the case). A chairman may give a contingent or hypothetical vote to come into operation if, in the course of subsequent proceedings, it should appear that there has been an equality of valid votes.[18]

Since a casting vote is conferred on the office of chairman, and not on the individual, it must be exercised as a fiduciary power in what the chairman considers to be the interest of the company as a whole.

(f) *To declare the result of voting.* Section 378(4) provides that, unless a poll is demanded, the chairman's declaration that an extraordinary or special resolution is carried is conclusive without proof of the number or proportion of the votes recorded for or against the resolution. Regulation 47 of Table A extends this principle to the voting on all resolutions by providing that, unless a poll is demanded, a declaration by the chairman that a resolution has been carried, carried unanimously, carried by a particular majority, lost, or lost by a particular majority and an entry made in the minutes to that effect is conclusive without proof of the number or proportion of the votes recorded for or against the resolution. A properly made and bona fide chairman's declaration under these provisions will prevent the question being reopened in legal proceedings even if evidence is forthcoming that the chairman's declaration was wrong.[19] The only exceptions to this are: first, where there is an apparent error, such as where the chairman states the number of votes given and they are insufficient[20] or where it is plain on the face of the proceedings that the requisite majority was not obtained;[21] secondly, where there is no apparent opposition to a proposal, but the chairman omits to put it to a show of hands, as required by Table A, reg 46.[22]

Under reg 58 of Table A the chairman has the final and conclusive power to decide on the qualification of any person to vote at a company meeting. In the absence of bad faith or fraud, the court will not interfere with the exercise by the chairman of this power.[23]

Finally, it should be noted by way of a proviso to the foregoing that no decision of the chairman will be conclusive if it relates to a resolution that was not in accordance with the notice for the meeting. In *Betts & Co v MacNaghten*,[24] it was held that notwithstanding a declaration by the

---

18 *Bland v Buchanan* [1901] 2 KB 75.
19 *Arnot v United African Lands* [1901] 1 Ch 518.
20 *Re Caratal (New) Mines* [1902] 2 Ch 498.
21 *Re Clark & Co* [1911] SC 243.
22 *Re Citizens Theatre Ltd* [1946] SC 14.
23 *Wall v London & Northern Assets Corporation (No 2)* [1899] 1 Ch 550; *Wall v Exchange Investment Corporation* [1926] Ch 143.
24 [1910] 1 Ch 430.

chairman, the notice of the meeting is part of the proceedings and may be looked at to see if the resolution is in accordance with it. If it is not, the chairman's declaration that the resolution was passed is not conclusive. Neither is a chairman's declaration conclusive where there is no quorum, since there would be no properly constituted meeting.

CHAPTER 16

VOTING AT MEETINGS

General principles

Voting at meetings generally takes place either on a show of hands or on a poll. The articles of association usually set out the voting rights attached to the shares. Insofar as they do not, s 370(6) applies and gives members, in the case of a company originally having a share capital, one vote for each share or £10 of stock, and in any other case one vote for every member. Although the Act is not specific on this point, s 370(6) presumably applies only to a vote on a poll.[1]

It is common for the articles to deal with these matters and reg 54 of Table A, for example, provides that, subject to any other rights or restrictions attached to the shares, on a show of hands every member present in person and holding shares entitled to vote at the meeting shall have one vote, and on a poll every such member shall have one vote for each share of which that member is the holder. Articles in this form are also consistent with s 372(2)(c) which provides that, subject to the articles, a proxy has a vote only on a poll. Even if, however, the articles provide that a member present by proxy may vote on a show of hands the proxy will only have one vote on the show of hands whether a member of the company or not.[2]

Under case-law, it is clear that the right of an alien enemy to vote personally or by proxy in respect of shares in an English company is suspended during war.[3] At a more quotidian level, articles frequently provide that certain classes of shares, for example preference shares, shall confer no vote at general meetings or shall confer a right to vote at such meetings only on certain specified matters or when the preference dividend is in arrears for a certain period. Most forms of articles also contain a restriction on the right of a member to vote unless all calls or other sums presently payable by the member in respect of shares in the company have been paid (for example Table A, reg 57).

It used to be common to find provisions in articles stating that a member was not entitled to exercise votes in respect of shares until that member had held them for a specified period. In other cases, voting rights were exercisable by a

1 *Ernest v Loma Gold Mines* [1897] 1 Ch 1.
2 Ibid.
3 *Robson v Premier Oil & Co* [1915] 2 Ch 124.

member only upon a limited number of shares; thus, if the member held more than that number, he or she had no (or reduced) voting rights in respect of the excess. Neither of these restrictions is common today, but they are still found on occasions.

As between the company and a member, a member may vote as that member pleases (provided the member has not been disqualified by the articles or the Act). Even if the company is aware that the member is, or may be, under a contract with a third person (including another member) to vote in a certain way or as that other person directs, the company is not entitled to question or reject a vote cast by a member in accordance with the articles.[4] This does not mean, however, that the court, if applied to, would not restrain the exercise of such a vote. There are two general classes of cases in which the court will constrain a shareholder to exercise his or her vote in a way dictated by another person. The first class involves certain circumstances in which a member holds shares in which another person has an interest. For example, in the absence of a contract a person in whose name shares are registered, such as a mortgagee, may vote as that person pleases, but where the mortgagee of shares agrees for a valuable consideration to vote at general meetings of the company in accordance with the wishes or the mortgagor, the court will enforce the agreement by mandatory injunction.[5] Similarly, an agreement made by a shareholder who has sold his or her shares, to vote in a particular way until the share transfer is registered, is valid and can be enforced,[6] and a member who holds shares as nominee or bare trustee for another is bound to vote as the beneficial owner directs.[7] On the other hand, in the absence of express provisions to the contrary, an unpaid or partly paid vendor of shares, remaining registered in respect of them, retains the right to decide how those shares should be voted.[8] The other class of cases (of considerable commercial importance) in which a shareholder's right to exercise his or her vote will be constrained by an obligation to a specified third party is where that shareholder has entered into a voting agreement with other shareholders to vote in a certain way on a certain issue.[9] However, the company may not be a party to such a contract.[10]

Subject to these types of contractual and equitable restrictions in favour of other specified persons, members may use their vote as they please. They are not subject to a fiduciary duty and motive is immaterial. 'There is no obligation on a shareholder of a company to give his vote merely with a view to what other persons may consider the interests of the company at large. He has a right, if he thinks fit, to give his vote from motives or promptings of what he considers his

---

4 *Siemens Bros v Burns* [1918] 2 Ch 324.
5 *Puddephatt v Leith, No 1* [1916] 1 Ch 200.
6 *Greenwell v Porter* [1902] 1 Ch 530.
7 *Wise v Lansdell* [1921] 1 Ch 420.
8 *Musselwhite v CH Musselwhite* [1962] Ch 965.
9 *Russell & Northern Bank Development Corporation Ltd* [1992] 1 WLR 589.
10 Ibid.

own individual interest.'[11] This rule is itself, however, subject to the qualification that a majority of the members will not be allowed by the exercise of their votes to commit a fraud on the minority.[12] This means, in effect, that a member must not vote so as to give that member, or that member and others, something which belongs to or ought to belong to the company.[13] Nor may a member vote in a way which benefits that member, or that member and others in their capacity as members, in a way which is detrimental to the interests of other members[14] or which differentiates them, unless, of course, the other members all agree. This qualification on the general rule becomes of greater significance in the case of meetings of a class of members. 'While usually a holder of shares or debentures may vote as his interests direct, he is subject to the further principle that where his vote is conferred on him as a member of a class he must conform to the interest of the class itself when seeking to exercise the power conferred on him in his capacity of being a member.'[15] One of the most important applications of this qualification is found when members of one class are also members of another class. Such members may not exercise votes at one class meeting to benefit themselves as members, perhaps to a greater extent, of the other class. In all these cases the court will not interfere to restrain or set aside votes unless it is clear that the member was exercising the votes improperly. If there has been full explanation of the proposal, and it is supported by members with no different interests, the courts will be slow to conclude that the votes of members who had other interests were not validly cast.

Articles normally contain restrictions on the power of directors to vote at board meetings on contracts or arrangements in which they are interested.[16] No such restrictions apply to them when they vote in their capacity as members at general meetings,[17] but their duty as directors requires full disclosure to the members of any different interest which they may have.[18]

Articles also usually contain regulations for voting by joint holders of shares, and in cases of members of unsound mind (regs 55 and 56 of Table A are examples). Further, articles frequently provide that no objection may be raised to a voter except at a meeting at which the voter tenders a vote, and the articles make the chairman of the meeting the person who decides upon any such objection (see, for example, reg 58). This is an awkward and in one

---

11 *Pender v Lushington* (1877) 6 ChD 75. For an extreme application of this principle, see *Northern Counties Securities v Jackson and Steeple Ltd* [1974] 1 WLR 1113.

12 *Menier v Hooper's Telegraph Co* (1874) LR 9 Ch 350.

13 For examples see *Menier v Hooper's Telegraph Co*, above, *Cook v Deeks* [1916] 1 AC 554.

14 *Clemens v Clemens Bros Ltd* [1976] 2 All ER 268.

15 *British America Nickel Corporation v O'Brien* [1927] AC at 373; *Goodfellow v Nelson Line* [1912] 2 Ch 324; *Re Holders Investment Trust Ltd* [1971] 1 WLR 583.

16 See regs 85 and 86 of Table A and s 317.

17 *East Pant-Du United Mining Co v Merryweather* (1864) 2 H&M 254.

18 In addition, the approval of a general meeting is required for any substantial property transaction between a director and the company: see ss 320 to 322B.

respect possibly a misleading provision. It is awkward because very often other members who might well wish to object may be unaware that a particular person has voted, or may not then know of a conflicting interest which that person has. It is misleading in the sense that if a member has voted for improper reasons the court will interfere, if asked, despite the wording of the article. On the other hand, such an article does seem to mean that objections to the *qualification* of a voter must be taken at the meeting – where they may be answered – and not later. Every vote not disallowed is valid and the chairman's decision is conclusive whether or not his or her mind was directed to the point by an objection.[19]

Show of hands

Unless the articles otherwise provide, voting will in the first instance normally be by show of hands. As stated above, usually every member personally present and entitled to vote has one vote only on a show of hands, independent of the number of shares or proxies that person holds. At a meeting of the members of a company, the articles of which allow voting by proxy, the chairman, in ascertaining the number of votes given on a show of hands, must count the vote of each member who holds proxies as a single vote, and not count a vote for each of the members whose proxies are held by that person.[20] The vote of a non-member, that is a person not entitled to vote on his or her own account but who is a proxy for a member, will not, unless the articles so provide, be counted on a show of hands (s 372(2)(c)). Regulation 54 of Table A does not so provide. A representative of a corporation, however, under s 375 would be entitled to vote on a show of hands by virtue of sub-s (2) of that section. Regulation 54 also envisages the vote on a show of hands by a duly authorised representative of a corporation. Due to the restrictions on non-members voting on a show of hands, it is desirable that if non-members are admitted to the meeting they should be known to the chairman to prevent them taking part in such a vote. Similarly, if members not entitled to vote are entitled to attend, the presence of such members should be brought to the attention of the chairman.

Regulation 46 of Table A provides that at any general meeting a resolution put to the vote of the meeting shall be decided on a show of hands, unless a poll is (before or on the declaration of the result of the show of hands) validly demanded and most articles contain a similar provision. In such a case, it is not necessary to go through the procedure of a show of hands. The chairman, or the appropriate number of members, may demand a poll as soon as the resolution is put, or may demand it beforehand. However, the virtue of a show

---

19 *Marx v Estates & General Investments Ltd* [1975] STC 671.
20 *Ernest v Loma Gold Mines Co* [1897] 1 Ch 1.

of hands, particularly where there is a bitter proxy battle, is that it enables those who have taken the trouble to attend in person to express their feelings, even though these may have no effect on the result of the motion. Regulation 47 of Table A makes the chairman's declaration on a show of hands conclusive.

Demanding a poll

The articles may contain provisions governing the way in which a poll must be demanded at any general meeting, but all such provisions will be subject to the provisions of s 373 which is overriding. The effect of this section is that:

(a) articles cannot exclude the right to demand a poll (except on the election of the chairman of a meeting or on the adjournment of a meeting); and
(b) articles cannot make a demand ineffective if made by
  (i) at least five members entitled to vote, or
  (ii) members holding 10 per cent or more of the voting rights of all the members having the right to vote at the meeting, or
  (iii) members holding shares on which 10 per cent or more of the total paid up capital has been paid.

The section also provides that a proxy may demand or join in demanding a poll (sub-s (2)). (See also reg 46 of Table A.)

Modern articles usually provide that the chairman of a meeting may demand a poll, and they sometimes provide that members fewer in number or smaller in holdings than the minimum specified in s 373 may demand a poll. For example, reg 46 of Table A empowers the chairman to demand a poll, and it also permits two members having the right to vote and present in person or by proxy to demand a poll.

If a poll is duly demanded it is the chairman's duty to grant it, and to fix the time and place for the poll in accordance with the articles. This power is a fiduciary power and must be exercised in a reasonable way to enable the members to record their votes. It would not, for example, be reasonable or proper to direct that the poll be taken at midnight on a Saturday, or in a place where shareholders could not conveniently attend.

If the demand is challenged it must, of course, be justified, but it need not be justified if the chairman knows privately that the demand is, in fact, supported by the requisite number.[21] In such a case, it is usually simpler and preferable for the chairman to resolve the point by making the demand. If a poll is not taken after a proper demand for a poll has been made, the resolution which has been challenged is void.[22]

The articles may provide, as does reg 48 of Table A, that the demand for a poll may be withdrawn with the consent of the chairman, in which case any pre-existing vote on a show of hands will remain valid.

---

21 *Re Phoenix Electric Light Co* (1883) 48 LT 260.
22 *R v Cooper* (1870) LR 5 QB 457.

Taking a poll

Articles frequently provide that a poll demanded on the election of a chairman or a question of adjournment is to be taken forthwith, but that a poll on any other question is to be taken at such time as the chairman directs, and that business other than that on which the poll is demanded may proceed in the meantime (see, for example, reg 51 of Table A). By reg 49, a poll is to be taken in such manner as the chairman directs (except as provided in reg 51) and the result of the poll is to be deemed to be the resolution of the meeting at which the poll was demanded.

It is, under s 373, competent for articles to provide that no poll may be demanded on the election of a chairman or on a question of adjournment. Accordingly, articles sometimes provide that the election of the chairman or a motion for an adjournment be determined on a show of hands of those members present at the meeting. In such cases, numbers present, and not shares held, are decisive. More usual, however, are articles in the form of reg 51 of Table A providing for any poll to be held immediately on these two questions. For motions on which the articles provide that the chairman shall decide when and how the poll be taken, the chairman's power of decision is a fiduciary one. If the chairman thinks that, in order to obtain the considered views of shareholders, the poll should be fixed for a future date, of which notice can be given, he or she should follow this course. If, on the other hand, the chairman thinks that the matter is too urgent for that course, or that shareholders have already had the opportunity to express their considered views, the chairman should hold the poll as soon as possible.[23] The decision is the chairman's, not the board's. Where the articles provide that a poll shall be taken within seven days of the meeting, at a time and place to be fixed by the directors, such time and place must be fixed after a poll has been demanded and cannot be fixed in advance.[24]

The usual method for taking a poll is to require every member who is entitled to vote to sign a paper (in order to prevent impersonation) headed 'for' or 'against' the motion; the number of votes to which each member is entitled under the articles is inserted against the signature of the member, and these having been added, the chairman declares accordingly.

A member may vote personally at a poll even if he or she was not present when the poll was demanded.[25] If, as is usual, the articles provide that a proxy is effective if deposited a certain number of hours before the taking of a poll, a shareholder who had not previously attended or appointed a proxy may appoint one for this purpose.

Resolutions must be put to the poll separately and not en bloc, otherwise the

---

23 See *Re Chillington Iron Co* (1885) 29 ChD 159.
24 *Re British Flax Producers Company* (1889) 60 LT 215.
25 *Campbell v Maund* (1836) 5 A&E 865.

poll is invalid.[26] All the resolutions may, however, be included on one sheet of paper, to be separately marked by the voters.

Scrutineers are often appointed to be present at the counting. Regulation 49 of Table A, for example, provides that the chairman may appoint scrutineers who need not be members. It seems, in any case, that where the articles do not provide for the appointment of scrutineers, they may be appointed by the chairman. Unless the articles require scrutineers, it is not obligatory to have any; but it is advisable for two reasons. First, the presence of independent scrutineers reduces the danger of a poll being subsequently challenged by a dissident shareholder, and secondly, because if, as is usual, the auditors are appointed, they have the staff and experience necessary for conducting the poll. Sometimes where there is a dispute, scrutineers representing the warring parties are appointed jointly, but dissident shareholders have no right to insist on the presence of scrutineers appointed by themselves. There is no duty of confidence on scrutineers or organisers of the poll in relation to the way in which votes are cast, as it is necessary to know how votes are cast in order to determine the validity of the poll.[27]

The right to vote and the number of shares held are determined by reference to the register of the members. 'The register of shareholders, on which there can be no notice of a trust, furnishes the only means of ascertaining whether you have a lawful meeting or a lawful demand for a poll, or of enabling the scrutineers to strike out votes.'[28] Where there is a limitation on the number of votes which any member may exercise, the member may transfer some of his or her shares to trustees on his or her behalf and, if they are duly registered, increase his or her voting power.[29]

The chairman should fix the hours during which the poll is to take place. If the chairman does not do so, he or she cannot close the poll so long as votes are coming in. After waiting a reasonable time, if no more voters present themselves, the chairman may declare the poll closed. The improper exclusion of a voter may invalidate a poll.[30]

Unless the articles specifically provide to the contrary (which Table A does not), a poll cannot be taken by sending voting papers to the members, to be lodged with the company. They or their proxies must attend and give the votes personally.[31]

Section 374 provides that on a poll a member entitled to more than one vote need not use all his or her votes or cast all the votes used in the same way. The object of this provision is to enable a person holding shares as trustee, proxy or

---

26 *Patent Wood Keg Syndicate Ltd v Pearse* (1906) WN 164.
27 *Haarhaus & Co GmbH v Law Debenture Trust Corp plc* [1988] BCLC 640.
28 *Pender v Lushington* (1877) 6 ChD 70, 78.
29 *Re Stranton Iron and Steel Co* (1873) LR 16 Eq 559.
30 *R v Rector etc of St Mary, Lambeth* (1838) 8 A&E 356.
31 *McMillan v Le Roi Mining Co* [1906] 1 Ch 331.

nominee for more than one person to vote as he or she is instructed, even if different instructions require him or her to vote in different ways.

A poll is regarded as part of the proceedings of the original meeting. 'The taking of a poll is a mere enlargement of the meeting at which it was demanded.'[32] The poll is complete from the day when the result is ascertained and declared, and not from the end of the voting.[33]

Proxies

The word 'proxy' is used confusingly to describe a person appointed in the place of another to represent him or her, and also the instrument by which such a person is appointed. The right to appoint a proxy is conferred by s 372(1). Under that subsection, a member entitled to attend and vote at a meeting is entitled to appoint another person, who need not be a member of the company, as a proxy, to attend and vote instead of the member. With respect to a private company, the subsection also confers on the proxy the same rights to address the meeting as enjoyed by the member appointing the proxy. The subsection does not apply to a company not having a share capital and in that case the right, if any, to appoint a proxy must be conferred by the articles (s 372(2)(a)). Unless otherwise provided by the articles, a proxy may vote only on a poll (s 372(2)(c)). Table A does not otherwise provide and consequently the position arises that a proxy may count towards a quorum under reg 40 (see Chapter 15), but may not vote unless a poll is demanded. As already noted, a proxy has, under s 373(2), the same right to demand or join in demanding a poll as the person who appointed the proxy would have had.

Section 372(2)(b) also provides that a member of a private company is not entitled, unless the articles so provide, to appoint more than one proxy to attend on the same occasion. In public companies the right is to appoint one or more proxies. This means that a member could in theory appoint one proxy for each share that he or she holds. It does not have the restricted meaning of appointing one person, or failing that person, another, and so on.

The expenses incurred by a board in sending out proxies are properly payable by the company. Indeed the Listing Agreement of the Stock Exchange requires companies whose shares are listed to send out proxies for all resolutions to be proposed. In *Peel v London and North Western Railway Co*,[34] it was held that it was the duty of the directors to inform the shareholders of the facts of their policy, and the reason why they considered that this policy should be maintained and supported by the shareholders, and that they were justified in trying to influence and secure votes for this purpose, and accordingly that

---

32 *R v Wimbledon Local Board* (1882) 8 QBD 464; *Shaw v Tati Concessions* [1913] 1 Ch 292.

33 *Holmes v Keyes* [1958] Ch 670. Whether a declaration of the result is strictly necessary is not clear, but it would be difficult, for example, for newly elected directors to act unless they know the result of the vote.

34 [1907] 1 Ch 5.

expenses which had thus been bona fide incurred in the interest of the company were properly payable out of the funds of the company. These expenses included the issuing of stamped proxy papers containing the names of three directors as proposed proxies with a stamped envelope for return. This is an important decision in relation to take-over bids and in cases where a group of shareholders is attacking the directors, for it enables directors to use the company's funds to defend their policy. By virtue of s 372(6), invitations to appoint a person or persons as proxy, if issued at the company's expense, must be sent to all members entitled to vote at the relevant meeting. Failure to observe this rule lays every officer of the company knowingly or wilfully authorising or permitting the default open to a fine. However, a proviso to the subsection makes it clear that no liability will attach to officers who issue to a member, at the member's request, a proxy form or a list of persons willing to act as proxy, provided that the form or list is available to all members entitled to vote.

The Act does not specify any particular form of proxy. Table A offers two types: one where there is an open discretion to the appointee as to how to vote (reg 60); the other where the proxy is directed how to vote (the 'two-way' form) (reg 61). The Stock Exchange requires, for listed companies, the latter form.

Proxy battles have increased in England in recent years, and some of the difficulties which arise could be avoided by a more carefully worded form of proxy. For example, the form should make clear whether the proxy may exercise any discretion on an amendment, or on a motion to adjourn the meeting. These points can be important if, as is usually the case, the proxy appointed is one of the directors, who may represent a large number of shareholders and may be uncertain as to his or her powers. In some cases, the proxy's course of conduct will be easy to decide,[35] but on other occasions the proxy may be unclear as to what he or she can and should do.

The proxy may even find him- or herself in a position where he or she believes that, in the interests of the person by whom the proxy was appointed, the vote should be used in a way different from the direction given in the form of proxy. For example, the proxy may have been directed to vote in favour of a scheme which the directors had recommended, but now finds that a more favourable scheme is offered. In such a case, it seems that the proxy may not vote contrary to his or her authority, but may probably refrain from using the vote altogether, unless under some contractual or fiduciary obligation to the member, for example as the member's solicitor. In that case, the proxy must in principle exercise the vote, as he or she is obliged and not merely authorised. It is sometimes suggested in addition that those who solicit proxies (as directors will frequently do) thereby impose upon themselves such an obligation. This is not clear. It may seem an unduly inflexible control, but if it is otherwise, the protection given to members by the two-way proxy (which in any event is

---

35 See *In re Waxed Papers Ltd* [1937] 2 All ER 481.

incomplete since the member will usually have heard only the directors' side of the argument) will become largely illusory, as directors would merely exercise those proxies favourable to them. Where a proxy holder purports to vote in a manner contrary to the instructions given in the proxy form, without any apparent justification for so doing, the chairman or scrutineers should note specifically the proxies concerned, and if the figures affect, or could affect, the result of the resolution, application should be made to the court to determine whether the votes be accepted as cast, accepted as the form of proxy directed, or rejected.

Two conflicting principles of law arise in connection with proxies, and a chairman may sometimes find it difficult to decide whether to accept or reject a vote which a person claims to exercise as a proxy. The first principle is that it is the duty of the chairman to obtain, if possible, the decision of the shareholders. The second is that, since the right to appoint a proxy is given by contract, that is, the contract constituted by the articles, any member who seeks to exercise the right to appoint a proxy must carry out and comply with whatever the articles specify. In accordance with the first principle, it has been decided[36] that where articles prescribed that proxies must be in a specified form or as near thereto as circumstances should permit, and the specified form was a proxy applicable to a single meeting, general proxies were permissible.

On the other hand, where particular formalities are prescribed they must be followed. If they are not, it is not merely the chairman's right, but his or her duty, as representing the shareholders, to reject them. One formality usually required by the articles is that forms of proxy be deposited with the company in advance of the meeting. The usual requirement is for the deposit to be made not less than 48 hours before the meeting (see, for example, reg 62 of Table A). The Act prohibits a longer period from being specified (s 372(5)). The importance of strictly complying with formalities specified in the articles as to place or time of deposit or the form of address on an envelope is illustrated by *Burnett v Gill*.[37] In this case, the articles provided that no person should be entitled to vote as a proxy unless the instrument appointing that person was deposited at the office of the company 48 hours before the meeting. The company's registered office was the office of the secretary, a chartered accountant. It was held that a proxy addressed to 'The Chairman of the Meeting, c/o The Secretary' whose name only was mentioned, was not duly deposited at the office.

In *Harben v Phillips*,[38] Cotton LJ explained the principle which justifies requiring compliance with formalities in the articles: 'The right of a shareholder to vote by proxy depends on the contract between himself and his co-shareholders, and where parties have a right depending upon the contract between them and the other parties, then, in my opinion, all the requisitions of

36 *Isaacs v Chapman* (1915) 32 TLR 183.
37 (1906) *The Times*, 13 June.
38 (1883) 23 ChD 14 at 32.

the contract as to the exercise of the right must be followed.' In that case, it was held that the proxy papers which were not attested as required by the articles were improperly admitted by the chairman. Presumably, even though the right to appoint a proxy is now conferred by the Act, the articles may still validly require attestation of the proxies. If they do, the person appointed as proxy cannot act as an attesting witness.[39]

Articles may provide that a vote given in accordance with the terms of an instrument of proxy is to be regarded as valid, notwithstanding the death or insanity of the principal, or revocation of the proxy or authority under which it was executed, or the transfer of the share under which it was given, unless notice of the event giving rise to the invalidity is received at the registered office before the meeting or adjourned meeting at which the proxy is to be used. In *Cousins v International Brick Co*,[40] the articles contained a similar provision, but it was held that a shareholder who had given a proxy and had not revoked it could attend the meeting personally and vote, in which case his proxy could not vote for him. The provision for revocation by a transfer is a dangerous one: in order to give it any meaning, the word 'transfer' must mean something less than registration. If so, sending of a transfer form to the company constitutes notice of the transfer and the result will be that, until the transfer is registered, the shares concerned may be disenfranchised. The transferor remains on the register but is treated as having revoked any proxy which he or she had given previously. The transferee may be unable to obtain a fresh proxy from the transferor, who by that time will probably not be concerned as to whether the votes are exercised or not.

Difficult problems frequently arise as to which of two or more proxies is valid. It is sometimes thought that a later proxy automatically revokes an earlier one, but this is not so. There are two facets to the problem: the first, what was the intention of the appointor; the second, what is the evidence of the intention. As to intention, it will normally be the intention of a person who makes a new appointment that a former appointment be revoked and replaced by the new one, but this will not necessarily be the case. The appointor may forget about the earlier proxy; the appointor may intend that both appointments should be effective, perhaps in order to increase his or her voting rights; the appointor may think that he or she is required to fill up the form which has been sent to him or her; or the appointor may wish to confuse the matter for the sake of confusion. As to the evidence of the intention, there is usually none except perhaps a date on the form of proxy or the date when it is received. But with modern postal delays, date of receipt is little guide, and dates on the forms themselves are by no means conclusive. The matter may be further complicated if an earlier proxy is stated to be irrevocable, or if the company is on notice that it was given, irrevocably, for valuable consideration.

The problem should be avoided as far as possible by some provision in the

---

39 *Re Parrott* [1891] 2 QB 151.
40 [1931] 2 Ch 90.

articles, but in the absence of that, the following guidelines are offered to enable a chairman or scrutineer to decide on proxy problems, where the problem is not covered by the articles:

(a) If there are two or more proxies for the same shares, the later in date (if given) should be accepted to the exclusion of the earlier.

(b) If there is no date, the one which appears on the evidence to have been signed later should be accepted to the exclusion of the others.

(c) If there is no sufficient evidence, and both proxy holders claim the right to vote, they should both be excluded since neither can establish the right.

(d) If a later proxy is received too late to be used at the meeting, it will, nevertheless, constitute notice of revocation of the earlier proxy. If the meeting is adjourned, or a poll is held later, the later proxy may be valid for that purpose.

(e) If the earlier proxy, in any of the above cases, was made irrevocable for valuable consideration and the proxy holder claims that he or she is still entitled to the vote, that claim should be recognised as being the valid compliance with the requirements of the articles for voting by proxy. A shareholder must not be assumed to intend to commit a breach of the contract with the earlier proxy holder, and any later proxy should be rejected so long as the first proxy holder claims the right to vote.

(f) If the shareholder is personally present at the meeting, this presence will not of itself revoke the authority given to the proxy. If the shareholder seeks to vote, this will displace his or her proxy on that resolution, but the authority revives for subsequent purposes unless, once again, the shareholder acts to displace the proxy's authority.

It has been decided that if the articles provide that a proxy shall be valid, notwithstanding that it has been revoked, unless notice of revocation is received before the meeting then that provision shall mean what it says. Accordingly, a revocation notice received after the commencement of the meeting but before a poll is taken is ineffective.[41] If, however, the shareholder votes in person, this will constitute valid revocation.[42]

A proxy for a specified meeting is not available for a different meeting. This will be so even if the specified meeting never takes place and another meeting is called instead, perhaps for identical business. A similar type of issue arose in *Oliver v Dalgleish*[43] where forms of proxy were given to X by a number of shareholders for a meeting to be held on a particular day. The forms described the meeting as an annual general meeting whereas it was in fact an extraordinary general meeting. Some of the forms instructed X to vote against the resolutions. X simply marked his voting paper 'for' the resolutions without stating how many votes he cast. The chairman rejected all his votes. It was held

---

41 *Spiller v Mayo* [1926] WN 78.
42 *Cousins v International Brick Co Ltd* [1931] 2 Ch 90.
43 [1963] 1 WLR 1274.

(a) that the misdescription of the meeting did not invalidate the forms of proxy, and (b) that the failure to obey the instructions of some of those who gave the proxies did not invalidate all the votes cast by X, who should be taken to have cast in favour of the resolutions all those votes which he was authorised so to use. The more difficult question, as to what to do with the votes instructed to be cast against the resolution, did not arise since they were insufficient to affect the outcome of the vote.

An adjourned meeting, as regards notice, is regarded in law as a continuance of the original meeting.[44] Consequently, where the articles require proxies to be lodged before the meeting this means the original meeting.[45] Normally, articles require the lodging before the meeting or adjourned meeting at which the votes are sought to be cast. In that case, lodging by the specified time before the adjourned meeting meets is effective; but this is only effective if the meeting is in fact adjourned. *Shaw v Tati Concessions*[46] makes it clear that if all that happens is that directions are given for a poll to be taken at a later time, but the meeting itself is not adjourned, the provision does not take effect so as to validate the proxy. The mere postponement of the poll is not an adjournment ad hoc of the meeting within the meaning of an article allowing the lodgement of proxies 48 hours before a meeting or adjourned meeting. The original meeting continues for the purpose of the poll, and no fresh proxies may be lodged.

The problem of *Shaw v Tati Concessions* will not arise where the articles permit lodging of proxies a certain period of time before the taking of a poll (rather than a certain period of time before the meeting). Articles frequently provide that proxies may be lodged not less than 24 hours before a poll (see, for example, Table A, reg 62(b)(c)). If this is so, there may be proxies which were too late (within 48 hours before the meeting) for effect in full at the meeting, for example to join in demanding a poll, but which are in time for being used if a poll is demanded and held.

---

44 *Scadding v Lorant* (1851) 3 HLC 418.
45 *McLaren v Thomson* [1917] 2 Ch 261
46 [1913] 1 Ch 292.

CHAPTER 17

TYPES OF RESOLUTIONS

Introduction

There are three types of resolution which may be taken in a company meeting: ordinary, extraordinary and special. It should be noted, however, that companies may also pass resolutions without a meeting. This may occur where a company passes a resolution by an informal corporate act or where a private company passes a resolution under the elective regime introduced by the Companies Act 1989.

Ordinary resolutions

Ordinary resolutions are usually referred to in the Act as resolutions of the company in general meeting, and are those which are passed by a bare majority of those voting at any kind of general meeting.

As has been pointed out, the articles may allocate certain powers to the board of directors in such a way that those powers can no longer be exercised by the company in general meeting. Apart from acts which have been thus assigned to the board, a company may carry out by ordinary resolution all such acts as are not required by the Act or by its articles to be effected by special or extraordinary resolution. There are, however, a number of things which a company is expressly empowered by the Act to carry out by resolution of the company in general meeting, that is, by an ordinary resolution. For example, s 121 provides in certain cases that the company in general meeting may, if so authorised by its articles, make certain changes to the conditions in its memorandum. Changes in capital structure, for example, (not including reduction) are permitted under this section. The fact that the Act gives such power does not mean that the articles may not require something more stringent, and the articles of private companies frequently provide that changes in capital require a special resolution.

The one case in the Act where there is specific reference to an ordinary resolution is s 303, which provides that a company may by ordinary resolution remove a director before the expiration of the director's period of office, notwithstanding anything in its articles or in any agreement between the company and the director. Special notice is required of any resolution to remove a director under this section or to appoint at the same meeting a director to replace the director so removed. The meaning of special notice is considered below.

On receipt of notice of an intended resolution to remove a director under s 303 the company is bound forthwith to send a copy of the notice to the director concerned, and the director (whether or not a member of the company) is entitled to be heard on the resolution at the meeting (s 304(1)). The company is also obliged to circulate representations in writing by the director or to allow such representations to be read out at the meeting (s 304(2) and (3)). This provision on directors' representations is subject, however, to the court being satisfied, on the application of the company or any other aggrieved person, that the circulation of the director's representation is not being used in order to secure needless publicity for defamatory material (s 304(4)).

Although s 303 requires that special notice be given of a resolution to remove a director under the section, it does not require that the resolution be proposed by the person who gave the special notice. Once someone has given special notice, that person or any other shareholder entitled to vote may propose the resolution. It is to be noted that the Act does not itself authorise the appointment of some other person in place of a director removed in this way; this is left to the articles. All that is provided in this respect is special notice of any intention to appoint someone else, and that if a vacancy caused by a removal is not filled at the meeting it may be filled as a casual vacancy (s 303(3)), which again leads back to the articles to discover who has the power to fill the vacancy and how. Where the vacancy is filled at the same meeting at which the director is removed then the person so appointed is, for the purpose of ascertaining which directors are to retire by rotation, deemed to have been appointed on the day the removed director was last appointed a director (s 303(4)). So far as the director who has been removed at the meeting is concerned, the section does not deprive that director of compensation or damages payable in respect of the termination of his or her appointment as director or of any other appointment terminating with the appointment as director, for example as managing director, and is not to interfere with any other power that the company may have of removing a director (s 303(5)).

The provisions of s 303 override anything to the contrary in the articles. Subsection (5) makes it clear, however, that the procedure for removing a director in s 303 is not the only procedure which may be used by the company. It seems that the power in s 303 is additional to any other powers which the company may have to remove a director. Thus, provisions in company articles which provide for removal of a director by, for example, extraordinary resolution, may be used by the company without the need for compliance with any of the requirements of ss 303 and 304, including the requirement of special notice. Likewise, it seems to be the case that if the articles provide for removal by ordinary resolution, such a provision may be relied upon to the exclusion of the requirements in ss 303 and 304.

In private companies, or companies of special types, the provisions of ss 303 and 304 are sometimes contrary to what the shareholders want or what is in their true interests. In such cases, special articles are often incorporated which give special protection to the directors. The classic example of this occurred in *Bushell v Faith*, in which the House of Lords upheld the validity of an article giving extra votes to a director on a resolution to remove that director.[1] Despite what Lord Morris said in that case, such articles are sometimes important or even essential in order to safeguard the interests of persons who may, for example, have incorporated a company to be operated as a quasi-partnership. On the other hand, larger companies would have little legitimate use for such a provision, and no listed company could have such an article.

Special notice

Special notice of an ordinary resolution is required by the Act in three classes of cases. One of these relates to the removal of a director under s 303, the provisions of which are discussed immediately above. The other circumstances in which the Act requires special notice for a resolution relate to the position of the auditor and the appointment of a director over the age of 70. In relation to auditors, special notice is required for: a resolution to fill a casual vacancy in the office of the auditor (s 388(3)(a)); a resolution to reappoint a retiring auditor who was appointed by the directors to fill a casual vacancy (s 388(3)(b)); a resolution to remove an auditor before the expiration of the auditor's term of office (s 391A(1)(a)); and a resolution appointing as auditor a person other than a retiring auditor (s 391A(1)(b)). So far as the appointment of a director over the age of 70 is concerned, s 293(5) provides that special notice must be given of a resolution appointing such a person as a director of a public company or a private company which is a subsidiary of a public company (including a Northern Ireland public company.) (The election of directors and auditors is further discussed in Chapter 18.)

The special notice required in the case of resolutions of the three cases just mentioned is dealt with by s 379, which provides that, where special notice is required of a resolution, the resolution shall not be effective unless notice of the intention to move it has been given to the company not less than 28 days before the meeting at which it is moved, and the company shall give its members notice of any such resolution at the same time and in the same manner as it gives notice of the meeting or, if that is not practicable, shall give them notice, either by advertisement in a newspaper having an appropriate circulation or in any other way allowed by the articles, not less than 21 days before the meeting.

A proviso (s 379(3)) lays down that if, after notice has been given to the company, a meeting is called for a date 28 days or less after the notice has been

---

1 [1970] AC 1099.

given, the notice though not given within the time required by the section shall be deemed to have been properly given for the purposes thereof. This achieves the dual purpose of ensuring first, that the directors cannot frustrate the proposal by promptly calling a meeting without the removal resolution, and, secondly, of making effective a resolution for removing a director even if, for convenience or to save expense or by necessity, the meeting is called for holding within the specified 28 days.

It will be noted that the requirements as to special notice are twofold. First, notice of the intention to move the resolution must be given to the company not less than 28 days before the meeting at which it is to be moved, and consequently even if the board desire to put forward a resolution for which special notice is required, they must arrange for someone to give this notice to the company. This notice should be given by a person who, being entitled to do so, intends to propose the resolution, but provided that such notice has been duly given, any member may in fact propose the resolution. Secondly, on receipt of this notice the board 'shall' give notice of the proposed resolution to the members in the same way as it gives notice to the meeting. This does not, however, confer on an individual member any right to compel the board to include the resolution in the agenda for a meeting, and is merely part of the machinery to ensure that members will have, subject to the proviso, at least 21 days' notice of a resolution requiring the special notice procedure.[2] The member who gives special notice to the company can insist on the resolution going into the agenda only if there is a provision to this effect in the articles or if the member can invoke s 376 (which is discussed in Chapter 14).

Receipt by the company of notice of an intention to move a resolution under this section does not, however, compel the company to hold a meeting. If the notice signifies the intention to move the resolution at the next meeting they need not give notice of it until the next annual general meeting is held, unless an extraordinary general meeting is either convened in the ordinary way or requisitioned under s 368 before the date for the annual general meeting. If, therefore, the next meeting is not an annual general meeting, it will be sufficient to give 14 days' notice of the resolution (s 379(3)). If, however, it is impracticable for notice of the intended resolution to be given in the same way as notice of the meeting is given, then in any case, subject, again, to the proviso in s 379(3), 21 days' notice thereof must be given either by advertisement in a newspaper or in any other way allowed by the articles.

The regime for elective resolutions for private companies in s 379A does not cover the matters in relation to which special notice is required. Similarly, the provisions in s 381A on written resolutions of private companies do not apply to resolutions removing a director under s 303 or removing an auditor before the expiration of the term of the auditor's office under s 391 (s 381A(7)). This does leave some scope for confusion about the application of the special notice

---

2 *Pedley v Inland Waterways Association Ltd* [1977] 1 All ER 209.

provisions to some types of written resolutions under s 381A and to the law on informal corporate acts. Further attention is given to these matters below.

Extraordinary resolutions

The Companies Act and the Insolvency Act 1986 (IA 1986) provide that certain actions may only be taken by extraordinary resolution. This is a right of the members, and cannot be excluded by the articles. Those actions which may only be carried out by extraordinary resolution are: resolving that a company shall be wound up on the grounds that it cannot by reason of its liabilities continue its business (IA 1986, s 84(1)(c)); sanctioning the exercise by the liquidator of certain powers in a members' voluntary winding up (IA 1986, s 165(2)(a)); and certain variations of class rights (s 125(2)). In addition, articles sometimes provide that certain actions, for example the removal of a director without going through the formalities or giving special notice, may be effected by extraordinary resolution.

Section 378(1) provides that an extraordinary resolution is one which has been passed by not less than three-fourths of such members, as being entitled to do so, vote in person or, where proxies are allowed, by proxy at a general meeting of which notice specifying the intention to propose the resolution as an extraordinary resolution has been duly given. This subsection deals only with voting on a show of hands. Unless the articles otherwise provide, which they very seldom do, only members personally present are counted on a show of hands, not those present by proxy. The position on a poll is dealt with by s 378(5), which provides that in computing the majority on a poll demanded on the question that an extraordinary resolution or a special resolution be passed, reference shall be had to the number of votes cast for and against the resolution. In summary, for a special or extraordinary resolution to be passed on a show of hands at least 75 per cent of the members voting must vote in its favour, and on a poll 75 per cent of the total votes validly cast (which will include votes cast by proxies) must be in favour of the resolution.

The notice of the meeting at which it is intended to propose a resolution as an extraordinary resolution must set out the exact words of the resolution or its entire substance, and also that it is intended to propose the resolution as an extraordinary resolution.[3] As noted in Chapter 14, under s 369 the length of notice of a meeting (other than the annual general meeting) for passing an extraordinary resolution by a company other than an unlimited company is 14 clear days, unless a shorter notice is agreed to in the manner specified in sub-s (3) of that section.

The relationship between the requirements for an extraordinary resolution and a resolution passed by an informal corporate act was considered in *Re*

---

[3] *McConnell v Prill & Co* [1916] 2 Ch 57.

Oxted Motor Company.[4] In this case, it was held that an extraordinary resolution for voluntary winding up might be passed by the unanimous consent of
all the members, even though no notice had been given. This is, of course,
consistent with the general principle underlying the doctrine of informal
corporate acts that all the shareholders can consent to any proposal within the
company's powers unless the Act imposes any outside restriction, such as the
consent of the court. It should also be noted that, quite apart from the doctrine
of informal corporate acts, it is possible for voting members holding 95 per
cent in nominal value of the shares or, where there is no share capital,
representing 95 per cent of the voting rights, to agree to short notice for an
extraordinary resolution (s 369(3) and (4)).

Special resolutions

Special resolutions are required by the Companies Act or the Insolvency Act
for various purposes, some of the more significant of which are:

(1) altering the articles (s 9);
(2) altering the objects clause in the memorandum or conditions in the
     memorandum which could have been in the articles of association (ss 4
     and 17);
(3) changing the company's name (s 28);
(4) disapplying members' statutory pre-emption rights (s 95);
(5) approving, where permissible, the provision of financial assistance for the
     purpose of shares or agreements for the purchase of its own shares by a
     private company (s 155);
(6) reducing capital (s 135);
(7) procuring the winding up of the company by the court (IA 1986,
     s 122(1)); and
(8) voluntarily winding up the company (IA 1986, s 84(1)(b)).

In addition, the articles may provide that the company is only able to do
certain things by special (or extraordinary) resolution.

Section 378(2) lays down the requirements for the passing of a special
resolution. These are the same as the requirements for the passing of an
extraordinary resolution, except that instead of 14 days' notice, 21 days' notice
is required, and the resolution must be specified in the notice as a special
resolution. The majority required is the same as for an extraordinary resolution, that is three-fourths of those entitled to vote on a show of hands or
three-fourths of votes cast on a poll. The provisions governing voting by show
of hands and poll, and on short notice (see s 378(3)), are the same for
extraordinary resolutions and special resolutions.

Pursuant to the doctrine of informal corporate acts, a special resolution may
be passed with no notice if all shareholders entitled to attend and vote agree to

---

4 [1921] 3 KB 32.

it.[5] Indeed, as discussed below, a meeting is not even necessary for the application of the doctrine of informal corporate acts.

Amendments to proposed resolutions

(1) Special and extraordinary resolutions

Unless all the members entitled to attend and vote agree, the basic rule is that no amendment may be made to a proposed special or extraordinary resolution.[6] The only special or extraordinary resolution which may, therefore, be passed is that specified in the notice for the resolution. The rule includes circulars accompanying such notices. In *Moorgate Mercantile Holdings Ltd*,[7] a derogation from this general rule was allowed. It was held that a special or extraordinary resolution 'as passed can properly be regarded as "the resolution" identified in the proceeding notice even though (a) it departs in some respects from the text of a resolution set out in such notice (for example by correcting those grammatical or clerical errors which can be corrected as a matter of construction, or by reducing the words to more formal language) or (b) it is reduced into the form of a new text which was not included in the notice, provided only that in either case there is no departure whatever from the substance.'[8]

(2) Ordinary resolutions

The position is less stringent in relation to proposed ordinary resolutions. Nevertheless, any amendment to an ordinary resolution must be within the scope of the notice convening the meeting. This principle has been interpreted broadly so that in *Betts & Co v MacNaghten*[9] where notice was given of a resolution to appoint three named directors, an amendment to appoint two additional directors was held to be valid. In that case, however, notice was given of the resolution with the addition of the words 'with such amendments as shall be determined on at the meeting'. Similarly, in *Choppington Collieries v Johnson*,[10] the articles provided that the election of directors in place of those retiring by rotation was not special business. Notice was sent out of an annual general meeting stating that the business was, inter alia, to elect directors (in the plural) and also stating that one retiring director offered himself for re-election. It was held that the meeting could appoint persons other than the

---

5 *Cane v Jones* [1981] 1 All ER 533.
6 *Re Moorgate Mercantile Holdings Ltd* [1980] 1 WLR 227.
7 [1980] 1 WLR 227.
8 Ibid.
9 [1910] 1 Ch 430.
10 [1944] 1 All ER 762.

retiring director to be directors up to the maximum number allowed by the articles. This is consistent with the principle that an amendment should not impose a greater burden on the company than the original motion.

A proposed amendment to an ordinary resolution need not be in writing unless the articles expressly provide, but it should be sufficiently definite.[11] The proposed amendment must be put to the meeting, but need not be seconded unless the articles specifically require this. 'If the chairman put the question without its being proposed or seconded by anybody, that would be perfectly good'.[12] A chairman is, therefore, not justified in refusing a motion or amendment because there is no seconder unless the articles expressly provide that all motions and amendments shall be seconded. If the mover of an amendment does not challenge the chairman's ruling that an amendment should not be put, that is not a waiver of the mover's right to impeach the resolution.[13]

Where the amendments number more than one, these should be put to the meeting in the order in which they affect the main question and then the main question in its original form or as finally amended should be put to the meeting. Strict adherence to the formality of putting motions and amendments is not essential, provided they are put to the meeting in such a way that those present understand what it is that they are called upon to decide.[14]

Elective resolutions

The Companies Act 1989 introduced an elective regime for private companies into the Act. Section 379A(1) provides that an elective resolution may be passed by a private company making an election to do any one of the following things:

(a) to remove or extend the duration of authority to allot shares (s 80A);
(b) to dispense with the laying of accounts and reports before the general meeting (s 252);
(c) to dispense with the holding of annual general meetings (s 366A);
(d) to reduce the majority required to authorise short notice of a meeting (ss 369(4) and 378(3)); and
(e) to dispense with the appointment of auditors annually (s 386).

An elective resolution may only be passed at a meeting of which 21 days' notice in writing is given, and for which the notice states that an elective resolution is to be proposed and also states the terms of the proposed elective resolution (s 379A(2)(a)). All members entitled to vote in person or by proxy

---

11 *Henderson v Bank of Australasia* (1890) 45 ChD 330.
12 *Re Horbury Bridge Coal Co* (1879) 11 ChD 109 at 118.
13 *Henderson v Bank of Australasia* (1890) 45 ChD 330 at 350.
14 *Ex parte Stevens* (1852) 16 JP 632.

must agree to the passing of the elective resolution (s 379A(2)(b)). Notwithstanding this stringent requirement, the elective resolution may be revoked by an ordinary resolution (s 379A(3)). It also ceases to have effect if the company becomes a public company (s 379A(4)).

The most obvious impact of this elective regime on the matters previously discussed is s 379A(1)(d) which allows an elective resolution to permit short notice for a meeting or for a special resolution to be agreed to by the holders of 90 per cent of those entitled to attend and vote or, where the company does not have a share capital, 90 per cent of the total voting rights at the meeting, rather than 95 per cent as stipulated in s 369(4) in relation to notice for meetings and s 378(3) in relation to notice for special resolutions.

Informal corporate acts and written resolutions

The common law doctrine of informal corporate acts and the statutory provisions for written resolutions by private companies co-exist, slightly uneasily, with each other. Section 381C(2)(b) seems to be intended expressly to preserve the common law doctrine.

The common law doctrine of informal corporate acts applies in theory to any type of company, but in practice will probably only be used by those companies with a relatively limited membership. As indicated earlier in this work, the effect of the doctrine is that, provided the matter is intra vires the company, the agreement of all members entitled to attend and vote at a company meeting is binding on the company.[15] No meeting is necessary.[16]

There is some confusion as to whether those entitled to be heard, but not to vote, at a company meeting must also assent in order for there to be an informal corporate act. This issue was raised in *Duomatic Ltd*[17] but, on the facts of the case, it was not necessary to decide it because the non-voting shareholders in question had no actual right under the articles to attend or to be heard at the meeting. Nevertheless, the case is not generally regarded as supporting the proposition that those with the right to attend and be heard must assent in order for there to be a valid informal corporate act.

What is clear is that an informal corporate act can achieve what may only otherwise be achieved by extraordinary[18] or special resolution,[19] without the need for any of the formalities normally associated with such resolutions. Whether an informal corporate act can cure the absence of special notice as required by s 379 is a more vexed question. On general principles, one might

---

15 *Parker & Cooper v Reading Ltd* [1926] Ch 975.
16 Ibid.
17 [1969] 2 WLR 114.
18 *Re Oxted Motor Co* [1921] 2 KB 32.
19 *Cane v Jones* [1981] 1 All ER 533.

have assumed the answer to be in the affirmative, but some doubt arises as a result of the fact that the provisions for special notice are intended to protect persons other than the shareholders and it may, therefore, be that their unanimous consent is not to the point.

Section 381A(1) allows a private company to do anything which might be done by a resolution in general meeting or by a resolution passed at a meeting of any class of members of the company by a written resolution signed by all members entitled to attend and vote at the meeting. It is not necessary for the signatures of the members to be on a single document (s 381A(2)). As noted earlier, a resolution removing a director before the expiration of their term of office under s 303 or a resolution removing an auditor before the expiration of their term of office under s 391 cannot be passed using this statutory written resolution procedure (s 381A(7)). Subject to this, the procedure may be used to pass any resolution, including a special, extraordinary or elective resolution (s 381A(6)). At the time of writing, s 381B requires a copy of written resolutions to be supplied to the auditors, who have seven days in which to require that the matter be dealt with by the company in general meeting (s 381B(2)). There are, however, proposals for the abolition of this effective veto by the auditors.

Some confusion exists about the relationship between s 381A and reg 53 of Table A, which allows for a resolution in writing without the exceptions and other requirements contained in ss 381A–381C. It is tentatively asserted that an article in the form of reg 53 provides an alternative method of passing a resolution to that laid down in ss 381A (rather than reg 53 being subject to the statutory regime for written resolutions in ss 381A–381C), but there is much dispute over this. It is to be hoped that the proposed statutory clarifications in this area will deal with this uncertainty.

The provisions for written resolutions in ss 381A–381C are, in some respects, narrower than the doctrine of informal corporate acts as they apply only to private companies and are subject to approval by the auditors. On the other hand, it is arguable that in two respects the statutory provisions for written resolutions cover wider ground than the common law doctrine of informal corporate acts. First, it may be that the power of the company to alter its share capital under s 121 cannot be exercised by an informal corporate act. The basis of this argument is the unusually specific provision in s 121(4) which provides that 'The powers conferred by this section must be exercised by the company in general meeting'. This may pre-empt the application of the doctrine of informal corporate acts, but it is generally thought that the wording of s 381A(1) would permit a private company to pass a written resolution under s 121. Secondly, s 381A(6) specifically includes elective resolutions within the ambit of the statutory procedure for written resolutions. It is, however, open to doubt whether an elective resolution could be effected by an informal corporate act. The reason for this doubt arises from the wording of s 379A(2)(b) which provides that the resolution must be 'agreed to at the meeting'.

Registration of resolutions

Section 380(1) requires that certain resolutions and agreements must be lodged with the Registrar of Companies within 15 days of their passing or making. The Registrar is obliged to record the relevant resolution. The same types of resolutions and agreements which must be lodged with the Registrar must also be embodied in, or annexed to, every copy of the articles issued after the passing of the resolution or the making of the agreement (s 380(2)).

The resolutions and agreements to which these provisions apply are listed in s 380(4). They include resolutions of the type listed below which are effected by an informal corporate act or by written resolution under s 381A. The resolutions in question are as follows: special resolutions; extraordinary resolutions; elective resolutions and resolutions revoking elective resolutions; resolutions of, or binding members of, a class of shareholders; resolutions passed by company directors in order to effect a change of company name on the direction of the Secretary of State under s 31(2); resolutions to give, vary, revoke or renew an authority to the directors for the allotment of certain securities under s 80; a resolution of the directors to alter the company memorandum on the company ceasing to be a public company under s 147(2); a resolution conferring, varying, revoking or renewing authority for a market purchase by the company of its own shares under s 166; a resolution for voluntary winding up under s 84(1)(a) of the Insolvency Act; and a resolution of the directors of an old public company that the company should be re-registered as a public company under s 2(1) of the Consequential Provisions Act.

Failure to comply with the provisions of s 380 as to lodgement with the Registrar and as to annexation to the articles makes the company and every officer in default liable to a fine (s 380(5) and (6)).

CHAPTER 18

BUSINESS OF MEETINGS

Introduction

The articles may provide that all business conducted at extraordinary general meetings, and all except certain specified matters to be conducted at annual general meetings, is to be special business; and the articles may further provide that notice of a general meeting is, in the case of special business, to specify the general nature of that business. Such provisions were found in regs 50 and 52 of Table A to the 1948 legislation. The business specified in reg 52 as not being special business of an annual general meeting consisted of the consideration of the accounts, balance sheets and reports of the directors and auditors, the election of directors in place of those retiring, and the appointment of, and the fixing of the remuneration of, the auditors. The result of an article such as this is to make it unnecessary to specify these matters, because they are not special business, in the notice convening the meeting. In the present Table A, however, there is no equivalent provision to reg 52. Accordingly, where the articles are in the form of the present Table A, all business to be transacted at an annual general meeting is, it appears, special business and must be specified in the notice.

Reading the notice

Meetings are usually opened by the secretary reading the notice convening the meeting, or the chairman asking the meeting to agree that the notice be taken as read. Even the latter is a somewhat pompous formality, and quite unnecessary. There is no statutory requirement to read the notice. It is far more sensible for the chairman or proposer of each resolution to read the proposed resolution when its turn comes, so that shareholders are aware at the relevant time of what they are considering. Sometimes the minutes of the previous meeting are then read and formally verified as correct, but, unless required by the articles, this proceeding at a general meeting is unnecessary and, generally, a waste of time.

Consideration of accounts etc

A private company may pass an elective resolution under s 252 to dispense with the laying of accounts and reports before the general meeting. In all other cases, s 241 requires the directors to lay before the general meeting (in practical terms, the annual general meeting) a copy of the profit and loss accounts and a balance sheet for each financial year. They may also be required to lay a copy of the group accounts (see s 227) before the meeting. This must be done within seven months (for public companies) or 10 months (for private companies) after the end of the 'relevant accounting reference period' (s 244(1)), which is effectively the end of the financial year (s 244(6)).[1] In addition, the auditor's report and the directors' report must be laid before the general meeting with the accounts (s 241). The requirements for the auditor's report are laid down in ss 235 and 236. In particular, it should be noted that under s 235(3) the auditors are required, if they consider that the information given in the directors' report for the relevant financial year is not consistent with the annual accounts for that year, to state that fact in their report. The requirements for the directors' report are found in ss 234 and 234A. These sections require, among other things, that the directors' report should contain a fair review of the development of the company's business and that of its subsidiaries during the financial year and state the amount (if any) recommended to be paid by way of dividend and the amount (if any) proposed to be carried to reserve (s 234(1)). There are, however, a number of other requirements for the directors' report contained in these sections and in Sch 7 to the Act. Failure to comply with all of these provisions is an offence (s 243(5)).

Under s 238(1), copies of the annual accounts together with copies of the directors' report and the auditor's report must be sent to every member of the company, every debenture holder of the company and to all other persons entitled to receive notices of general meetings of the company, for example the auditors, at least 21 days before the date of the meeting at which the documents are to be laid. They need not be sent to members or debenture holders who are not entitled to receive notices of meetings if the company does not know the addresses of such people; and if joint holders of shares and debentures are not all entitled to notices of meetings, copies need only be sent to those joint holders who are entitled to notices or, if none is entitled, to one such joint holder (s 238(2)). In the case of companies not having a share capital, these documents need not be sent to members or debenture holders who are not entitled to receive notices of meetings of the company (s 238(3)). All members may agree to copies being sent outside the time-limit of 21 days (s 238(4)), but in the absence of such agreement the company and every

---

1 As to the calculation of the company's financial year end and the 'accounting reference period', see ss 243 and 244.

officer in default commits an offence if there is failure to comply with the time-limit (s 238(5)).

The chairman usually begins by making some comments on the accounts, then he or she may explain the position of the company, giving such further information concerning its affairs as he or she thinks may properly be made known, and, finally, conclude by moving that the reports and accounts be adopted. This is usually seconded by another director with a few remarks, following which the members present at the meeting are free to comment on or criticise the reports, accounts and the chairman's speech. So far as it is possible without prejudice to the interests of the company, the directors should answer freely all inquiries regarding the accounts and the company's affairs. However, they are not bound to answer in general meeting any questions which they consider undesirable, in the best interests of the company, to answer.

Unless steps have been taken in advance by dissatisfied members, there is usually very little that the members can do at an annual general meeting if they are dissatisfied with the directors' report or the conduct of the directors. They can vote against the resolution for the adoption of the report, but even if the resolution is lost, this has no effect other than to indicate the disapproval of a majority at the meeting. If the resolution is lost, an attempt is sometimes made by the dissatisfied members to appoint a committee of inspection from among their number to look into the affairs of the company, but this cannot be done without proper notice of a resolution to this effect having been given. This procedure is, in any case, valueless, since the resolution does not give the committee any powers of investigation for requiring information. So long as the directors remain as the directors of the company, they retain their powers as such and the company cannot remove the control of its affairs from them.[2] In some cases, where the meeting proves hostile, the directors may agree to give certain information to a committee appointed by the dissatisfied members and to adjourn the meeting until that has been done. They are not, however, bound to do so.

Dissatisfied shareholders may also make an application to the Secretary of State to investigate a company under s 431, but only if they together number 200 shareholders or 10 per cent of the holders of the issued shares, or, where the company has no share capital, one-fifth of the persons on the register of members (s 431(2)). The applicants for such an investigation must give supporting evidence showing they have good reason for requiring an investigation (s 431(3)) and they may also be required to give security (s 431(4)). Even after all this has been done, there is no guarantee that an investigation will be ordered. The unpredictability of the outcome of applications for company investigations means that where the majority of members of a company disapprove of the conduct of the directors they are probably better off availing themselves of the power conferred by s 303 to remove the directors by

---

2 *Automatic Self-Cleansing Filter Co v Cunninghame* [1906] 2 Ch 34.

ordinary resolutions and appoint others in their place by like resolutions (see Chapter 17). This, however, can only be done if the requisite notices have been given, and if the notices have not been given in time for an annual general meeting, a subsequent meeting will have to be requisitioned for this purpose.

Declaring a dividend

Assuming the report is adopted, one of the directors usually then moves the payment of the dividend recommended therein. Articles usually provide that the company in general meeting may declare dividends, but that no dividend shall exceed the amount recommended by the directors, see, for example, Table A, reg 102.

Election of directors

The articles generally contain provisions relating to the retirement and election of directors. For example, Table A provides that at the first annual general meeting all the directors shall retire from office and at subsequent annual general meetings one-third of the directors (being those who have been longest in office) shall retire (regs 73 and 74). Table A goes on to provide that, at the meeting at which a director retires under the rotation provisions, if the company does not fill the vacated office, the retiring director if willing to act is deemed reappointed, unless it is resolved not to fill the office or a resolution for the retiring director's re-election is lost.[3] The intention to propose any person (other than a retiring director or a person recommended by the directors) for election to the board must, under reg 76, be given to the company with notice of the willingness to act of the person proposed to be elected. Regulation 76(a) provides that such notice must be given not less than 14 or more than 35 clear days before the meeting. Where the directors propose to recommend someone other than a retiring director for election to the position of director then, under reg 77, they must give notice of that fact to the company not less than seven or more than 28 clear days before the meeting. Subject to all these provisions, appointments under Table A to the office of director may be made by ordinary resolution (reg 78) and, for the period between annual general meetings, the board may (subject to certain provisos) appoint someone to be a director (reg 79).

In the case of a public company, the appointment of each director must, to be valid, be effected by a separate resolution unless the meeting agrees without a dissentient to a motion for the appointment of two or more directors being made by a single resolution (s 292(1)). A resolution moved in contravention of that section is void and the persons thereby intended to be appointed directors will not be so appointed (s 292(2)). The section also provides that if an

---

3 See *Grundt v Great Boulder Proprietary Gold Mines Ltd* [1948] Ch 145.

election is thereby avoided and the office of a retiring director is in consequence not filled, no provision for the retiring director's automatic reappoint-
ment such as in reg 75 of Table A referred to above is to apply (s 292(2)).

The position of auditor

The eighth EC Company Law Directive made provision with respect to the
eligibility of a person to become a company auditor. The requirements of the
Directive in this respect are implemented by Part II of the Companies Act
1989. Under these provisions, either an individual or a firm may be appointed
as a company auditor (s 25(2)), provided, of course, that they comply with the
other requirements as to eligibility, including the requirement of sufficient
independence in s 27. The provisions on appointment, removal and resignation of auditors are found in Part XI, Chapter V of the Companies Act 1985.
Under these provisions, only dormant companies are exempt from the obligation to appoint auditors (ss 384(1) and 388A). However, a private company
may resolve by elective resolution to dispense with the annual appointment of
auditors (s 386). It should also be noted that where a private company has
passed an elective resolution under s 252 to dispense with the laying of
accounts and reports before the general meeting, then s 385A modifies its
obligations in relation to the appointment of auditors.

Except in the case of a company which has elected to dispense with the
laying of accounts, a new company's first auditor may be appointed by the
directors to hold office until the end of the first general meeting before which
the accounts are laid (s 385(3)). In the case of a company which has elected to
dispense with the laying of accounts, the first auditor may be appointed by the
directors either before the period of 28 days beginning with the day on which
copies of the first annual accounts are sent to members under s 238 and until
the end of that period, or where a notice has been given under s 253(2)
requiring the laying of the accounts before the company in general meeting, at
any time before that meeting until the beginning of the meeting (s 385A(3)). If
the directors fail to appoint an auditor under these provisions, the company in
general meeting may do so (ss 385(4) and 385A(4)). Thereafter, every company must appoint auditors at each general meeting before which the accounts
are laid (s 385(2)), to hold office from the end of that meeting until the end of
the next such meeting. This obviously does not apply, however, to companies
which have elected to dispense with annual appointment under s 386. Nor
does it apply to companies which have elected to dispense with the laying of
accounts. In the latter case, auditors must be appointed before the end of the
period of 28 days, which commences with the day on which the accounts are
sent to the members, for a period running from the end of that 28-day period
until the next time for appointing auditors, or where notice has been given
requiring the laying of accounts before the company in general meeting,
before the conclusion of the general meeting to hold office from the conclusion

of the general meeting until the next time for appointing auditors (s 385A(2)).
If the company fails to make an appointment, it must give notice to the
Secretary of State, who may fill the vacancy (s 387). Should a casual vacancy
arise, the remaining auditors may continue to act and the directors or the
company in general meeting may appoint an auditor to fill the casual vacancy
(s 388).

The remuneration of auditors is fixed by the company in general meeting,
or in such manner as the company in general meeting may determine
(s 390A(1)). Where auditors are appointed by the directors or the Secretary of
State, their remuneration may be fixed by the directors or the Secretary of
State, respectively (s 390A(2)). (Section 390B governs remuneration of auditors for non-audit work.)

The company has power by ordinary resolution to remove an auditor before
the expiry of his or her term of office (s 391); however, such a resolution
requires special notice (s 391A). (Special notice is considered in Chapter 17.)
Notice that such a resolution has been passed must be given to the Registrar of
Companies within 14 days (s 391(2)). The removal is effective even though it
may amount to a breach of contract between the company and the auditor,
who in that case retains the right to compensation or damages for the termination of his or her appointment or of any other appointment which terminates
along with his or her appointment as auditor (ss 391(1) and (3)).

The requirement of special notice where the auditor is being removed,
either before the expiration of the auditor's term of office, or by virtue of
someone else being appointed in place of a retiring auditor (s 391A(1)) is part
of a number of requirements designed to bolster the independence of auditors.
For the same reason, special notice is also required in order for the company in
general meeting to fill a casual vacancy or to reappoint an auditor appointed by
the directors to fill a casual vacancy (s 388(3)). In summary, this means that
special notice will always be required for resolutions concerning the filling of
the position of auditor unless the resolution is merely to reappoint an auditor
appointed at the last general meeting or to reappoint the company's first
auditors appointed by the directors.

On receiving a resolution requiring special notice in relation to the position
of auditor, the company must forthwith send a copy of the resolution to the
person it is proposed to appoint or remove (ss 388(4) and 391A(2)). Where it
is proposed to appoint someone other than a retiring auditor to the position of
auditor or to remove an auditor before the auditor's term of office expires, the
retiring auditor or the auditor whose removal is proposed may make written
representations concerning the resolution to the company and may request
the company to notify its members of those representations (s 391A(3)). The
company must then state that representations have been received in any notice
of the resolution given to members and must send a copy of the representations to every member to whom notice of the meeting is or has been sent
(s 391A(4)); unless the representations are received too late to allow this to be
done. If the representations are received too late for inclusion in the notice sent

to members or the company fails to comply, the auditor may demand that the representations are read out at the meeting (s 391A(5)). This is subject to the usual proviso that the court may accede to the request of the company or an aggrieved person that the representations are not sent out or read at the meeting if it is satisfied that the rights are being used to secure needless publicity for defamatory material (s 391A(6)).

An auditor removed in mid-term by an extraordinary general meeting may attend and speak at the general meeting at which his or her term of office would normally have expired and any general meeting at which it is proposed to fill the vacancy caused by his or her removal (ss 391(4) and 390). The auditor must, accordingly, be given all relevant notices of, and other communications relating to, such meetings which any member is entitled to receive.

The right of an auditor whose position has been terminated to attend and speak at certain meetings is, in fact, an extension of the rights enjoyed by all auditors while in office to receive all notices and communications which members are entitled to receive, and to attend and be heard at general meetings (s 390(1)). Similarly, the auditors have rights in relation to the written resolutions of private companies (which resolutions are discussed in Chapter 17). These are: to receive all communications relating to such a resolution as are required to be supplied to a member; to give notice that the resolutions concern them as auditors and should be considered by a general meeting, or a meeting of a class of shareholders; to attend such a meeting; and to be heard at such a meeting with respect to the business which concerns them as auditors (s 390(2)). (Where an auditor is not appointed annually his or her position may be terminated in accordance with s 393.)

An auditor may resign by depositing written notice of resignation at the company's registered office (s 392(1)). The resignation will be effective only if it states that there are no circumstances connected with the resignation which the auditor considers should be brought to the attention of members or creditors, or if it contains a statement of such circumstances (s 392(1)). The company must send a copy of the notice of resignation to the Registrar of Companies within 14 days (s 392(3)) and, if the notice contains a statement of special circumstances which the auditor considers ought to be brought to the attention of members and creditors, the company must, within the same period, send copies to all members and creditors entitled to receive the accounts under s 238 or must apply to the court on the ground that the statement is being used to secure needless publicity for defamatory material (s 394(3)). If such an application to the court is made, the company must notify the resigning auditor (s 394(4)) and if the resigning auditor does not receive notice of any application within 21 days from the deposit of the statement at the registered office, the resigning auditor must lodge the statement with the Registrar of Companies within a further seven-day period (s 394(5)). Where an application is made to the court by the company and upheld, then the company must send a statement setting out the effect of the court order to everyone entitled to receive accounts, within 14 days of the court order (s 394(6)). Where, on the other hand, the court does not uphold the company's application, then the company must circulate the document as ordinarily required and notify the resigning auditor, who must in turn send a copy of the statement to the Registrar within seven days of receiving notice of the court order (s 394(7)). These provisions are designed to ensure, inter alia, that company members are not left in a state of ignorance about disputes involving matters affecting the company's financial management. Failure on the part of the resigning auditor, the company or any company officer to comply with the requirements concerning circulation of resigning auditors' statements in s 394 is an offence (s 394A).

In addition to the rights under s 394 concerning circulation of statements of resigning auditors to the effect that special circumstances exist, a resigning auditor who has delivered such a statement may give the directors, at the same time, a requisition to call an extraordinary general meeting to receive and consider the resigning auditor's explanation of those circumstances (s 392A(2)). The resigning auditor may also call on the company to circulate to members a written statement of those circumstances before the general meeting at which his or her term of office would otherwise have expired or before any general meeting at which it is proposed to fill the place vacated by the auditor or which he or she has requisitioned (s 392A(3)). The company must then in any notice of the meeting inform members that the statement has been made and, subject to the usual proviso concerning an application to the court in the case of allegedly defamatory matter (s 392A(7)), send a copy to every member to whom notice of the meeting is or has been sent (s 392A(4)) or, if it fails to do this, have the statement read out at the meeting (s 392A(6)). The period of notice for the meeting must not exceed 28 days, and the directors must proceed to convene the meeting within 21 days of deposit of the requisition, failure to do so being a criminal offence (s 392A(5)). The auditor is entitled to attend the relevant meeting, receive notices and documents relating to it, and speak at the meeting on the business concerning the auditor as a former auditor (s 392A(8)).

Special business

This can be transacted at an annual general meeting provided due notice has been given. There is no need to transact special business at an extraordinary general meeting, although this is often done.

CHAPTER 19

ADJOURNMENTS

General principles

Where no provision is made by the articles as to the adjournment of a meeting, the power of adjourning is vested in the meeting.[1] Motions for adjournment can generally be brought forward at any period of the meeting, and take precedence over any matter then under consideration. Usually, however, the question of adjournments is provided for by the articles, in which case the provisions of the articles must be followed. In the unusual situation where the meeting is in total disorder, so the views of the members cannot be ascertained, the chairman has an inherent power (whatever the provisions of the articles) to adjourn the meeting for a short time, taking steps, so far as possible, to ensure that all present know of the adjournment.[2] The way in which the chairman may exercise this inherent power, and the power of the court to adjourn a meeting, are discussed below.

Regulation 45 of Table A gives a common example of the type of provision which may be included in the articles with respect to adjournments. It provides that the chairman of the meeting may, with the consent of a meeting at which a quorum is present (and shall, if so directed by the meeting), adjourn the meeting from time to time and from place to place, but that no business is to be transacted at any adjourned meeting other than the business left unfinished at the meeting from which the adjournment took place. When a meeting is adjourned for 14 days or more, seven days' clear notice of the adjourned meeting is to be given specifying time, place and general nature of the business. Otherwise, notice is unnecessary. Under an article such as this the power for adjournment is given absolutely to the meeting. Sometimes, however, the articles provide only that the chairman may adjourn with the consent of the meeting, without providing that the chairman shall adjourn if directed by the meeting. In that case the chairman cannot adjourn without the consent of the meeting, but cannot be compelled to adjourn the meeting against his or her wishes.[3]

Articles (for example reg 51 of Table A) usually permit a poll to be called for

---

1 Cf *R v Grimshaw* (1847) 11 Jur 965.
2 *John v Rees* [1970] Ch 345; *Byng v London Life Association Ltd* [1989]] BCLC 400.
3 *Salisbury Gold Mining Co v Hathorn* [1897] AC 268.

a proposal to adjourn. In that event, the articles will generally provide that the poll be taken immediately, or, if they do not so provide in express terms, there must be an implied requirement for the purpose in order to give effect to the obvious intention. If a poll is taken, the proxy holders may be in doubt whether or not they can exercise their proxy votes, and if so, how. In some situations, it will be plain how they should exercise the votes, as being in the best interests of their appointors.[4] Sometimes, they will have been given specific directions for this purpose, but in other cases they may be in doubt. A proxy holder should act on the principle that he or she is an agent for the appointor, and, in the absence of express instructions, is entitled to act in whatever way he or she feels is in the interests of the appointor or accords with what the appointor would wish. If the proxy holder takes a decision in accordance with that view, held in good faith, it will not be open to successful challenge by the appointor, the company or anyone else. If the proxy holder feels unable to decide, he or she may take no action. The agency is in the proxy holder personally; even if the proxy was canvassed by the board, it is the proxy, and not the board, who has the right and duty to decide.[5]

The directors of a company, in the absence of express authority in the articles of association, have no power to postpone a general meeting of the company properly convened.[6] If they endeavour to exercise such a power, the shareholders can, if they think fit, meet at the place, time and day appointed by the notice and transact all the business which could properly be put before the meeting as convened. If the directors wish to postpone a meeting, the only way is to meet formally and to persuade the meeting to adjourn itself to a more suitable and convenient time.

It is common for directors to wish to postpone a meeting, either because circumstances have changed or changes are expected. In such situations they should, if time permits, inform shareholders of their intention to postpone the meeting and the reason for this, either by circular or, where time is too short, by newspaper advertisement. The purpose of notifying shareholders is to indicate that the meeting will be a mere formality and it will be a waste of the shareholders' time to attend the meeting.

Finally, it should be noted that a meeting may, in certain circumstances, be continued on a later date without any adjournment in the strict sense having taken place.[7]

Exercise of the chairman's power to adjourn

The power to adjourn, given to the chairman either by the articles or inherently, is a fiduciary one. The chairman is not entitled to adjourn a meeting

---

4 See *Re Waxed Papers Ltd* (1937) 2 All ER 481.
5 See further on proxies, Chapter 16.
6 *Smith v Paringa Mines* [1906] 2 Ch 193.
7 *Jackson v Hamlyn* [1953] 1 Ch 577.

capriciously before the business of the meeting has been transacted, and if the chairman purports to do so without good reason, the meeting may appoint another chairman and proceed with the business.[8] Similarly, the chairman may not adjourn to a place or time which would be unreasonable for shareholders. Since the chairman's power is fiduciary, it will sometimes be the chairman's duty to adjourn. If, for example, he or she believes that shareholders should be given an opportunity to reconsider a proposal, or to consider an alternative, or to review the matter in the light of changed circumstances, the chairman should exercise the power to adjourn and should explain why the power is so exercised.

The inherent power of the chairman to adjourn has recently been considered by the Court of Appeal in *Byng v London Life Association Ltd.*[9] The article considered in this case was consistent with reg 45 of Table A, that is, it gave the chairman, with the consent of a quorate meeting, the power to adjourn. The Court of Appeal held that, if it was not possible for the chairman to validly ascertain the views of the meeting, such an article would not interfere with the chairman's fundamental common law duty to ensure that all who are entitled to be heard and to vote are given the opportunity to do so and the chairman's consequential residual common law power to adjourn the meeting. The reason that it had become impossible to proceed with the meeting and impossible to ascertain the views of the members as to adjournment in *Byng's case* was that the meeting was being held in a series of rooms which were supposedly linked by audio-visual means. However, the audio-visual system broke down and it became impossible to communicate adequately between the rooms. While the Court of Appeal upheld the residual common law power of the chairman to adjourn in these circumstances, it held that it was not sufficient that the chairman merely exercised the power of adjournment in good faith. Rather, the power must be exercised upon the basis of the principles laid down in *Associated Provincial Picture Houses Ltd v Wednesbury Corporation*[10] for the proper exercise of a discretion. In the context of company meetings, this means:

'The chairman's decision will not be declared invalid unless on the facts which he knew or ought to have known he failed to take into account all relevant factors or reached a conclusion which no reasonable chairman, properly directing himself as to his duties could have reached.'[11]

On the facts of the case, the chairman's behaviour in adjourning the meeting had not conformed with this principle. The reason for this was that the chairman had neglected to take into account a number of matters relevant to the exercise of his discretion to adjourn. These matters included the objections

---

8 *National Dwellings Society v Sykes* [1894] 3 Ch 159.
9 [1989] BCLC 400.
10 [1948] 1 KB 223.
11 [1989] BCLC 400 at 419, per Browne-Wilkinson LJ.

of members to the adjournment of the meeting to that afternoon; the fact that any members unable to attend the adjourned afternoon meeting in person would not be able to vote by proxy since it was too late for them to lodge their proxies; and the fact that the chairman was wrong in believing that it was necessary for the company to pass a special resolution on that day.

The court's power to adjourn

There are circumstances in which the court has a power to adjourn a company meeting. Such a power may be exercised where, for example, circulars sent to shareholders by the directors with the notice of the meeting are misleading.[12]

Business at adjourned meetings

Section 381 provides that where a resolution is passed at an adjourned meeting of a company, or a similar meeting of the holders of any class of shares of a company, or of the directors of a company, the resolution shall for all purposes be treated as having been passed on the date on which it was in fact passed and shall not be deemed to have been passed on any earlier date.

The articles usually provide what business may be conducted at an adjourned meeting. Usually, only business which could properly have been transacted at the original meeting, had it not been postponed, can be transacted at the adjourned meeting (see, for example, Table A, reg 45). Sometimes, however, it is possible to transact business which could not have been transacted at the original meeting. Thus in *Catesby v Burnett*,[13] the articles provided that a member should not be qualified to be elected a director unless 14 clear days' notice of the intention to so elect the member was given to the company before the day of election. At the date of the annual general meeting there were two directors due for retirement, but the meeting was adjourned without any election of directors. Notice had been given 14 clear days before the adjourned meeting, and the two new directors elected at that meeting were held to be validly appointed, since the date of the adjourned meeting was the day of election. If the articles had provided for 14 days' notice before the meeting at which they were elected (rather than 14 days' notice before the day of election), the election would not have been valid.

For similar reasons, proxies will sometimes be available for use at an adjourned meeting where they would not have been available at the earlier meeting, as, for example, where they have to be deposited not less than 48 hours 'before meeting or adjourned meeting' (see reg 62(a) of Table A).

An adjourned meeting is in law the continuance of the original meeting,[14]

---

12 *Northern Counties Securities v Jackson* [1974] 1 WLR 1133.
13 [1916] 2 Ch 325.
14 *Scadding v Lorant* (1851) 3 HLC 418.

and a fresh notice is not therefore necessary,[15] unless the articles require such a notice to be given. Most articles do so provide where the adjournment is of some length (for example, Table A, reg 45).

---

15 *Wills v Murray* (1850) 4 Ex 843.

CHAPTER 20

MINUTES

The obligation to record minutes

Section 382(1) provides that every company shall cause minutes of all proceedings of general meetings and all proceedings at meetings of its directors and where it has managers, at meetings of its managers, to be entered in books kept for that purpose. (Note, in this context, should be taken of reg 100 of Table A which imposes upon the directors the obligation to ensure that minutes are kept of the proceedings of the company, any class of shareholders, the directors or any committees of directors.) Section 382A(1) requires that written resolutions under s 381A must be recorded, along with the signatures of the members, in the same way as the minutes of a general meeting of the company. Where a company has only one member, then s 382B(1) requires that member to provide the company with a written record of any decision taken by the member which might have been taken by the company in general meeting. However, failure to comply with this requirement in relation to single member companies does not affect the validity of any decision arrived at by the single member (s 382B(3)).

The right to inspect the minutes

Section 383(1) requires the minutes of proceedings of general meetings of a company to be kept at the registered office of the company and to be open to the inspection of any member without charge. The Companies (Inspection and Copying of Registers, Indexes and Documents) Regulations 1991 require the company to make the minutes available for at least two hours during business hours on each business day and to permit the person inspecting the minutes to take notes or transcribe the information. It should only be necessary for members to avail themselves of this right to take notes where urgent access to the information in the minutes is required. This is because s 383(3) entitles any member to be furnished with a copy of any such minutes within seven days of making a request to the company for such a copy. The same subsection allows the company to charge a fee for this purpose. This fee is prescribed in Sch 2 of the Companies (Inspection and Copying of Registers, Indexes and Documents) Regulations 1991 as 10p per 100 words or part thereof.[1] The company, and every officer, in default under the section, is liable to a fine (s 383(4)), and the court may make orders for inspection, or direct copies to be sent to the persons requiring them (s 383(5)). These provisions regarding the right to inspect minutes apply equally to minutes embodying written resolutions (s 382A(3)).

There is no requirement that minutes of directors' meetings be available for inspection by members of the company. A director is, by virtue of his or her office, entitled to see minutes of directors' meetings, but, in the absence of an express provision in the articles, shareholders have no such right. The reasoning behind this was expressed in 1859 as follows:

> 'It is highly proper that an inspection of the books containing the proceedings of directors should be obtained on special occasions and for special purposes: but the business of such companies could hardly be conducted if anyone, by buying a share, might entitle himself at all times to gain a knowledge of every commercial transaction to which the directors engage, the moment that an entry of it is made in their books ... the proposed daily and hourly inspection and publication of all their proceedings ... would probably ere long be found very prejudicial to shareholders.'[2]

However, the minutes should be accessible to directors and the secretary. Auditors also are entitled under s 389A to see the minutes for the purposes of audit.

In addition, minutes should be kept of committees of the board. These, like minutes of board meetings, should be available for inspection by all the directors, whether or not they were members of the committee. Even if the matter discussed was concerned with a particular director, or affairs in which that director was concerned, and the director was excluded from the committee for that very reason, he or she is entitled as a director to know what decision was taken.

The minute-books

As the minutes of general meetings are required to be open for inspection by the members and those of directors' meetings are not, separate books are generally kept for each class of minutes.

Section 722 provides that any register, index, minute-book or accounting records required by the Act to be kept by a company may be kept either by making entries in bound books or by recording the matters in question in any other manner, and that where any such register, index, minute-book or books of account is not kept by making entries in a bound book but by some other

---

1 It should be noted that those matters described here as being laid down in the Companies (Inspection and Copying of Registers, Indexes and Documents) Regulations 1991 are, of course, more likely to be subject to change than the provisions of the Act itself.

2 *R v Mariquita Mining Co* (1859) 1 E&E 289.

means, adequate precautions must be taken for guarding against falsification and facilitating its discovery. The company and every officer of the company who fails to take adequate precautions are liable to a fine and daily default fines in the case of continued contravention. Consequently, with proper precautions, minutes may now be kept in loose-leaf books.

Contents and significance of the minutes

(1) General principles

Section 382(2) provides that minutes of any meeting required to be kept by s 382(1) shall be evidence of the proceedings if purporting to be signed by the chairman of that meeting or by the chairman of the next succeeding meeting. Further, by s 382(4), where minutes have been made, in accordance with the provisions of the section, of the proceedings at any general meeting of the company or meeting of directors or managers, the meeting is to be deemed to have been duly held and convened until the contrary is proved, and all proceedings thereat to have duly taken place, and all appointments of directors, managers or liquidators are to be deemed to be valid. It is essential, therefore, that the minutes should contain an accurate record of all proceedings transacted and appointments made (see also Table A, reg 100). This is as true for directors' meetings as for company meetings.

> 'Directors ought to place on record, either in formal minutes or otherwise, the purport and effect of their deliberations and conclusions; and if they do this insufficiently or inaccurately they cannot reasonably complain of inferences different from those which they allege to be right.'[3]

A clear distinction should be carefully drawn between a report and a minute. The former chiefly consists of what was said, the latter consists of what was done or agreed upon, and its place of record is the minutes. Speeches and arguments at a general meeting may form the material of a newspaper report, but the resolution and decisions are the only proper material for the minutes. The minutes will only be evidence of those matters properly entered in them.

Although not required by the Act, minutes are sometimes read or, if previously circulated to the members, taken as read, at the next following meeting, and submitted for verification of their correctness. If regarded as a correct report of the proceedings by those members present at that meeting, they are signed by the chairman. If considered incorrect, they may be modified and then signed. The person who should sign the minutes in order to ensure that the minutes are evidence of proceedings at the meeting is the chairman of that meeting or the chairman of the succeeding meeting, whether present or not at the previous meeting (s 382(2)). The minutes need not, unless required by the articles, be signed at, or with the approval of, a meeting.

---

3 *Re Liverpool Household Stores* (1890) 59 LJ Ch at 615.

The signature of the chairman to minutes which embody the terms of a contract may be sufficient to satisfy the Statute of Frauds,[4] where the Statute requires contracts to be evidenced by a memorandum in writing.

Once minutes have been signed, they should not be altered or corrected internally. 'I trust I shall never again see or hear of the secretary of a company, whether under superior directions or otherwise, altering minutes of meetings, either by striking out anything or adding anything.'[5] If they are found to be incorrect the proper procedure is to add a further minute or note correcting the mistake, and for the chairman to sign that addition. In this way, anyone who reads them will know the correct position, whereas a minute containing alterations renders it uncertain whether the alterations were authorised. If the original minutes were approved at a later meeting, the addition should also be approved and a record made of it. For similar reasons, pages should not be removed from the minute-book, the pages of which should be numbered consecutively.

The fact that the minutes when duly signed are evidence of the proceedings casts a burden of proving that the minutes are incorrect upon those so alleging.[6] In order to discharge this burden, evidence may be given to show what in fact was done even if this contradicts the minutes, and evidence may be given of a resolution passed but not recorded in the minutes.[7] Articles sometimes provide that the minutes of a meeting if purporting to be signed by the chairman shall be 'conclusive evidence without any further proof of the facts therein stated'. According to the only reported decision on such an article, evidence cannot be given in such a case to contradict minutes so signed unless it can first be shown that the minutes have been written up fraudulently.[8] There is much doubt whether this decision is correct, and an article so framed is most inadvisable. It would in any case bind only a member of the company, and probably only when dealing with the company in the capacity as such.

The secretary should make the necessary notes as each meeting, whether general or of the board, proceeds, and subsequently write up the minutes in the minute-book. The secretary should take care that the record is absolutely impartial and free from ambiguity, that the exact account of what was actually agreed upon and nothing more is minuted, and that it is sufficiently detailed and complete, so that an absent member would be able to fully understand from the record what was done at the meeting.

(2) Board meetings

It is not essential to the validity of the exercise of the power of the directors that their decision should be embodied in formal resolutions, provided that the

---

4 *Jones v Victoria Graving Dock* (1877) 2 QBD 314.
5 *Re Cawley & Co* (1889) 42 ChD 209 at 226.
6 *Re Indian Zoedone Co* (1884) 26 ChD 70 at 77.
7 *Re Fireproof Doors* [1916] 2 Ch 142; *Re Pyle Works (No 2)* [1891] 1 Ch 173 at 184.
8 *Kerr v John Mottram Ltd* [1940] Ch 657.

minutes record the substance of the decision made.[9] Nevertheless, the record should be sufficiently clear for absent members of the board to follow the proceedings. The minutes should, therefore, record the names of the directors present. The names of other persons, if recorded, should be stated as being 'in attendance'. In the case of resolutions of directors not carried unanimously, it is desirable to record the names of those who voted for and against the resolution if there is a request for such a record. A director is not entitled to have a protest recorded in the minutes, but if the director votes against a motion he or she is entitled to have that fact noted in the minutes.

It is generally desirable that the minutes of directors' meetings should not be signed until approved by a subsequent meeting. If a succeeding meeting of any kind requires the minutes of a previous meeting to be altered before approving them as correct, some reference to this should be made in the minutes of the later meeting. A director who is present at a meeting of the board at which the minutes of a previous board meeting are confirmed, even though that director is a party to their confirmation, is not thereby made responsible for what was resolved upon at such a previous board meeting if the resolution has been acted upon before the minutes are confirmed.[10] Such a director is, however, thereby given notice that such resolution was passed.

Finally, it should be noted that s 382(3) deems a declaration by a shadow director under s 317(8), made through a member of the board, that that shadow director has an interest in a company contract, part of the proceedings at a directors' meeting. Accordingly, such a declaration ought to be noted in the minutes of the meeting.

---

9 *Re Land Credit Co* (1869) LR, 4 Ch App 460 at 473.
10 *Re Lands Allotment Co* [1894] 1 Ch 616 at 635; *Burton v Bevan* [1908] 2 Ch 240.

CHAPTER 21

MEETINGS OF DIRECTORS

Introduction

Section 282 provides that every company registered on or after 1 November 1929 (other than a private company) shall have at least two directors, and every company registered before that date and every private company shall have at least one director.

Normal day-to-day management decisions are taken by directors and others with responsibility in that field delegated by the board. Some matters must be dealt with in a more formal way, with a record kept of any decisions, and for this purpose board meetings are held. Almost invariably, the articles contain provisions relating to board meetings. For example, reg 88 of Table A provides that, subject to the other articles, the directors may regulate their meetings as they think fit; that questions arising at any meeting shall be decided by a majority of votes; that in case of an equality of votes the chairman shall have a second or casting vote; that a director may, and the secretary on the requisition of a director shall, at any time summon a meeting of the directors; and that it shall not be necessary to give notice of a meeting of directors to any director for the time being absent from the UK. Further regulations on the proceedings of directors are contained in regs 89 to 98, and some of these are discussed below.

In considering the activities of directors discussed in this chapter (and in this book generally), it should always be borne in mind that directors hold their powers in a fiduciary capacity and must exercise them bona fide for the benefit of the company, not for their own ends.[1]

Chairman

To constitute a valid board meeting the proper person must be in the chair.

The appointment of the chairman is generally governed by the articles. Regulation 91 of Table A, for example, provides that the directors may elect a chairman of their meetings and determine the period for which the chairman is

---

1 *Piercy v S. Mills & Co* [1920] 1 Ch 77.

to hold office, and that if no such chairman is elected, if the chairman is unwilling to preside, or if at any meeting the chairman is not present within five minutes after the time appointed for holding the meeting, the directors present may choose one of their number to be chairman of the meeting.

The election of a chairman may be a general one or merely for a particular meeting. It is important that a clear record of this is kept in the minutes, since confusion and dispute will often result if it is not clear whether there is a regular chairman, especially if the articles give the chairman a casting vote. Moreover, confusion may be compounded by the fact that reg 91 requires no particular formality for the resignation of the chairman.[2]

An appointment of a chairman of directors made in contravention of the articles is void and is not regularised by mere acquiescence, and consequently resolutions carried by the casting vote of such a chairman are inoperative.[3]

Proper constitution of the board

Subject to what is said below concerning s 35A, acts done as directors by persons who have not been validly elected do not bind the company.[4] It may be otherwise if the fact that they were not properly elected is only discovered afterwards, for s 285 provides that the acts of a director or manager shall be valid notwithstanding any defect that may afterwards be discovered in his or her appointment or qualification. This section is merely intended to cure slips in the appointment of directors and cannot in any case be relied on by a person who in fact knew of the invalidity even if its discovery was not general, or when there was no appointment at all.[5]

Outsiders are, in the absence of knowledge to the contrary, entitled to assume that the domestic affairs of a company are properly conducted, the basis for this principle being known as the rule in *Royal British Bank v Turquand*.[6] It is outside the scope of this book to consider the present importance of this rule, but it seems that it is of minimal importance since the introduction of s 35A. The reason for this is that s 35A makes the acts of the directors binding on the company in favour of a person dealing with it in good faith, notwithstanding any constitutional limitations on the directors' powers. Knowing that an act is beyond the power of the directors does not show bad faith (s 35A(2)(b)). The effect of this provision seems to be to make concerns about the proper constitution of the board relevant in most cases only to internal disputes and then subject only to s 285.

Sometimes articles provide for alternate or substitute directors to act for directors going abroad. Under normal articles, one person may be alternate for

2 *Cane v Jones* [1981] 1 All ER 533.
3 *Clark v Workman* [1920] 1 IR 107.
4 *Garden Gully United Mining Co v McLister* (1875) 1 App Cas 39.
5 *Morris v Kanssen* [1946] AC 459.
6 (1856) 6 E&B 327.

more than one director, but it may be thought desirable to exclude such a possibility by expressly stating that one person may not be alternate for more than one director. An alternate director is counted as a director, and if the alternate is a director in his or her own right he or she counts as two persons, both for the purposes of quorum and of voting. Depending on the articles, it may be possible for one person to constitute a meeting if that person is duly appointed alternate for a sufficient number of directors to form a quorum.

Directors' obligation to meet

Where board approval is required, directors must either act at a duly consti-tuted meeting or by unanimous decision arrived at informally.[7] This require-ment of a board meeting was illustrated starkly in *Barber's Case*.[8] The articles provided that no person not recommended by the board of directors for election as a director should be eligible unless at the time that person had held 20 shares for two months. B, who was not a shareholder, was elected unani-mously at a general meeting, six out of seven directors, who were then the only shareholders, being present. It was held that B's election was void. 'Six directors out of seven met in a different capacity and for a different purpose, and such a meeting does not make them a board of directors.'[9]

A board meeting can be held under informal circumstances but, for example, a casual meeting of the only two directors of a company at a railway station cannot be treated as a board meeting at the option of one against the will of the other.[10] The dividing line is, however, narrow. Where one of the only two directors did not attend a meeting, proper notice of which had been given, but was met by the other director shortly after in the passage, that other director proposed a resolution and, on the first director objecting, declared it passed by virtue of his casting vote, and this resolution was held to have been duly passed.[11] In any case, a subsequent meeting can ratify the business done at an informal meeting.[12] It can also ratify an unauthorised act of an agent of the company.[13]

Articles frequently allow the directors, if unanimous, to act without holding a meeting. Regulation 93 of Table A provides that a resolution in writing, signed by all the directors entitled to receive notice of a meeting of the directors, shall be as valid and effectual as if it had been passed at a meeting of the directors duly convened and held.

---

7 *Collie's Claim* (1871) 12 Eq 246, 258; *Ex p Kennedy* (1890) 44 ChD 472 at 481.
8 *Re East Norfolk Tramways Co, Barber's Case* (1877) 5 ChD 963.
9 Ibid at 697.
10 *Barron v Potter* [1914] 1 Ch 895.
11 *Smith v Paringa Mines* [1906] 2 Ch 193.
12 *Re Portuguese Consolidated Copper Mines* (1889) 42 ChD 160.
13 *Molineaux v London, Birmingham etc Co* [1902] 2 KB 589.

A director need not attend every meeting, though he or she should attend as often as circumstances permit. A director is bound to use fair and reasonable diligence in the management of the company's affairs and to act honestly.[14] A director is not, however, liable for misfeasance committed by co-directors without his or her knowledge at a board meeting at which he or she is not present.[15]

Notice of meetings

Directors of a company can, at any meeting of the board, deal with all the affairs of the company then requiring attention so far as the powers conferred on them by the articles extend; previous notice of special business is not necessary[16] unless the articles so require.

Reasonable notice must be given of the meeting, but it need not be in writing unless the articles so provide.[17] Even in the absence of a provision such as that contained in reg 88 of Table A, presumably any director may summon a meeting. What is reasonable notice will depend on the facts in any particular case and may depend on a course of conduct. In *Re Homer Gold Mines*,[18] a shorter notice than any previously given was held invalid, since the court came to the conclusion that the notice had been so given with a view to excluding certain directors. A notice may, however, be extremely short if all the directors are able to attend and if any director wishes to object to the shortness of the notice that director should make such an objection at once.[19]

It might well be thought that failure to give proper notice to each director will invalidate all proceedings at the meeting (unless all the directors do attend).[20] But although the matter is not free from doubt, it seems that a director who does not receive proper notice merely has the right to a second meeting if that director does not attend the first; that the failure of that director to seek a second meeting within a reasonable time of discovering the first will amount to a waiver of that right; and that in this event the proceedings of the meeting become effectively unchallengeable.[21] There is, however, no need to send notice when the directors have decided to hold meetings at regular intervals, that is, when there is a fixed day and time of which all directors have knowledge, and therefore, notice (for example, weekly meetings on Fridays at

---

14 *Re Forest of Dean Coal Mining Co* (1878) 10 ChD 450; *Re City Equitable Fire Insurance Co* [1925] Ch 407.
15 *Perry's Case* (1876), 34 LT 716.
16 *La Compagnie de Mayville v Whitley* [1896] 1 Ch 788.
17 *Browne v La Trinidad* (1887) 37 ChD 1.
18 (1888) 39 ChD 546.
19 *Browne v La Trinidad* (1887) 37 ChD 1.
20 *Re Homer Gold Mines Ltd* (1888) 39 ChD 546; *Harben v Phillips* (1883) 23 ChD 14.
21 *Browne v La Trinidad* (1887) 37 ChD 1 (10 minutes' notice not specifying the business); *Bentley-Stevens v Jones* (1974) 1 WLR 638 (notice sent of meeting the following day and not received because director away from home until the evening of that day).

3 pm or every first Thursday in the month at 11 am). Even in the absence of a provision as to directors out of the UK similar to reg 88 of Table A, in certain circumstances notice need not be given to a director who is abroad and out of reach.[22] A director cannot, however, waive in advance his or her right to notice and even if the director says, 'I shall not be able to come, you need not summon me', he or she must be given notice.[23]

Quorum

(1) General rules

Business can only be validly transacted by the majority of the directors at a meeting properly convened[24] and held, and at which there is a quorum as prescribed by the articles. Regulation 89 of Table A provides that the quorum necessary for the transaction of the business of the directors may be fixed by the directors, and unless so fixed shall be two. Under a provision such as this, one director who is also alternate for another could constitute a quorum for a meeting. The articles may also provide that one director can constitute a quorum in any case.[25] If no provision on quorum is made by the articles, a majority of the directors will constitute a quorum, but under certain circumstances apparently the necessary number may be determined by the practice of the board.[26]

A quorum of directors means a quorum competent to transact and vote on the business before the board. Therefore, in *Yuill v Greymouth Point Elizabeth R Co*,[27] where the articles prohibited interested directors from voting, a resolution passed at a meeting of three directors, two of whom were interested in the subject matter of the resolution, was held invalid. In *Re North Eastern Insurance Co*,[28] articles provided that directors could contract with the company, but should not vote in connection with such contracts, and that until otherwise determined three should be a quorum. Four directors were present at a meeting. At that meeting a resolution was passed for the issue of a debenture to one of the directors present, who did not vote on that resolution, and a similar resolution was passed to issue another debenture to another director who was present, but did not vote on this latter resolution. It was held in the circumstances of the case that the issue of both debentures was part of one entire transaction in which the directors to whom the debentures were issued were jointly interested and that there was therefore no quorum and the debentures were not validly issued. It was subsequently resolved that in future

---

22 *Re Halifax Sugar Co* (1890) 62 LT 564.
23 *Re Portuguese Consolidated Copper Mines* (1889) 42 ChD 160.
24 *York Tramways Co v Willows* (1882), 8 QBD 685.
25 *Re Fireproof Doors* [1916] 2 Ch 142.
26 *Regent's Canal Ironworks* [1867] WN 79.
27 [1904] 1 Ch 32.
28 [1919] 1 Ch 198.

a quorum should be two so as to remove the difficulty. One of the directors interested in the transaction was one of the three directors present when that resolution was passed and being interested was unable to count towards a quorum. The purported reduction of the quorum was consequently in-effective. The principle that those who are not entitled to vote on a resolution at a board meeting cannot form part of the quorum is embodied in reg 95 of Table A, although these cases make it clear that the principle stands even in the absence of such an article.

(2) Abuse of quorum provisions

It seems that in certain circumstances the court will be prepared to step in and make an appropriate order where a director refuses to attend and thus deprives the board meeting of a quorum. An example of this occurred in *Re Copal Varnish Co*,[29] where one director out of a board of two refused to attend meetings summoned to consider transfers of shares in order to prevent a quorum being formed. It was held that the transferees were entitled to an order directing the company to register the transfers, since a shareholder has a property in his or her shares which he or she has the right to dispose of subject only to an express restriction in the articles. Even if the articles give directors a power to decline to register a transfer, such a power is not exercised where the directors have not passed a resolution declining so to register.[30]

(3) Failure to keep quorum

Where there is a quorum at the beginning of a meeting, but some of the directors leave the meeting, so that a number less than the quorum remain, any subsequent acts are invalid. This would not be the case if the articles provided that 'the quorum shall be two directors present when the meeting proceeds to business', as was found in relation to general meetings in *Re Hartley Baird*,[31] but such a provision would be most unusual. The normal provision is similar to that found in reg 89 of Table A referred to above.

(4) Minimum number of directors

Articles usually fix what is to be the maximum and minimum number of the directors. Where a minimum is fixed, and the number of the directors has never reached the minimum, they cannot act even though they are sufficient to form a quorum.[32] However, if there have been sufficient directors to satisfy the requirement of the minimum number, and their number falls below the minimum but there are nevertheless sufficient directors to form a quorum, the articles may provide that the directors are entitled to act (see, for example,

---

29 [1917] 2 Ch 349.
30 *Re Hackney Pavilion* [1924] 1 Ch 276.
31 [1955] Ch 143.
32 *Re Sly, Spink & Co* [1911] 2 Ch 430.

Table A, reg 90). However, where the number of remaining directors falls below the quorum then the articles generally give the continuing directors only very limited powers. Regulation 90 of Table A, for example, gives the continuing directors in these circumstances power only to fill vacancies or to call a general meeting. Under such an article, a single director may be entitled to act for those purposes.[33]

Directors' votes

(1) General

Unless the articles otherwise provide, each director has only one vote at a board meeting, and in the event of a disagreement the majority view will prevail, though the chairman is usually given a casting vote (see, for example, Table A, reg 88). In some circumstances, there may be a departure from the usual provision that decisions will be arrived at by a majority vote. For example, where there are special classes of shares each with rights to appoint directors, or where the company is, in effect, an incorporated partnership, articles frequently provide that all or some matters require an affirmative resolution from all directors, or from a specified majority, or from a majority including directors of both (or all) classes or factions.

(2) Votes of directors in matters of self-interest

Directors stand in a fiduciary relation to the company, and under the general rules relating to such a relationship a director cannot, in the absence of express provision in the articles, contract with the company without the sanction of the company in general meeting. A director is precluded from dealing on behalf of the company with himself or herself and from entering into any engagement in which he or she has a personal interest conflicting or which may possibly conflict with the interests of the company. This rule extends not only to contracts between the company and the director but also to contracts with any firms or companies in which that director has an interest either as director or shareholder and even if the director holds the shares in the other company as a trustee. The smallest conceivable conflict of interest will be sufficient to bring this rule into operation.[34] Even the allotment of shares or the issue of debentures by directors to themselves will fall within this rule [35] Most articles specify exemptions from this strict rule but frequently provide that in the case of any such contract the interested director is not to vote (for example, Table A, reg 94). In that case, a director prohibited from voting does not count towards a quorum (see, for example, Table A, reg 95). Such a prohibition will not, however, prevent a director from voting as a shareholder at general meetings

---

33 *Dover etc Light Railway Co* [1914] 1 Ch 568, 2 Ch 506.
34 *Transvaal Lands Co v New Belgium Land Co* [1914] 2 Ch 488.
35 *Neal v Quinn* (1916) WN 223.

of the company upon contracts in which that director is interested,[36] and a
director is entitled to attend board meetings even when that director is not
entitled to vote at the board meeting.[37] It is, however, perfectly competent for
the articles not only to permit such contracts but to allow the interested
directors to vote on connected matters.

Whether any such contracts are permitted by the articles or by the Act or
not[38] the provisions of s 317 must be observed. That section declares that it is
the duty of a director who is in any way, whether directly or indirectly,
interested in a contract or proposed contract or other arrangement or transaction with the company to declare the nature of his or her interest at a meeting
of the directors of the company (s 317(1) and (5)) and provides for a fine on
non-compliance with the section (s 317(7)). It is to be noted that it is not
sufficient for a director merely to declare the existence of an interest: the
director must declare the nature of the interest. This does not necessarily mean
the full extent or quantum of the interest. For example, if the interest that a
director has is 100 shares in the other contracting company, the director must
declare that he or she holds the shares but need not necessarily disclose the
number. If, however, the director's shareholding in the other company were a
controlling one, this fact would alter the nature of the interest held and the
director would have to disclose not merely that he or she is a shareholder, but
the controlling shareholder. The principle to be observed in deciding what has
to be disclosed is that any aspect of the interest which could or might affect the
attitude of the director or of the other members of the board, is part of the
'nature' of the interest and must be disclosed. The fact that a director discloses
the nature of an interest and does not vote does not absolve that director from
responsibility with regard to the proposal. The director is entitled to speak on
the proposal and if he or she feels it is against the interests of the company he or
she must say so. After having disclosed an interest, the director is not entitled
merely to sit back and wash his or her hands of the matter.

The section also provides that in the case of a proposed contract, the
declaration required by the section is to be made at the meeting of the directors
at which the question of entering into the contract is first taken into consideration, or if the director is not at the date of that meeting interested in the
proposed contract, at the next meeting of the directors held after the director
becomes interested, and in a case where the director becomes interested in a
contract after it is made, the declaration is to be made at the first meeting of the
directors held after the director becomes interested (s 317(2)).

Under the section, there is deemed to be a sufficient declaration of interest if

---

36 *North-West Transportation Co v Beatty* (1887) 12 App Cas 589.
37 *Grimwade v BPS Syndicate* (1915) 31 TLR 531.
38 It should be stressed that certain contracts between directors (or those connected with them)
   and their companies are, under the Act, either generally forbidden or tightly circumscribed
   (see, for example, the provisions in s 320ff on substantial property transactions involving
   directors; and the provisions in s 330ff on loans to directors).

the director gives the board a general notice that he or she is a member of a specified company or firm and is to be regarded as interested in any contract which, after the date of the notice, the company may make with that company or firm, or that the director is to be regarded as interested in any contract which, after the date of the notice, the company may make with a person connected with the director within the meaning of s 346 (s 317(3)).[39] But the notice has no effect until either it is given at a meeting of the directors or the director in question takes reasonable steps to secure that it is brought up and read at the next meeting of the directors after it is given (s 317(4)).

The provisions of s 317 also apply to shadow directors,[40] except that a shadow director must declare his or her interest by a notice in writing to the directors by either a specific notice in relation to a particular contract given before the date of the meeting at which a declaration would have been required by a de jure director in the same circumstances, or in the case of a general notice of interest, in the same way as required by other directors (s 317(8)).

Apart from any specific exemptions found in the articles (see, for example, Table A, reg 94) which permit a director to vote despite his or her other interests, articles usually provide in addition that the prohibitions may at any time be suspended or relaxed to any extent, and either generally or in respect of any particular contract, arrangement or transaction, by the company in general meeting (see reg 84 of Table A). However, even if the articles permit a director to vote on a resolution in which that director is interested, this does not absolve the director from disclosure, under s 317 of the nature of the interest. That disclosure has to be made so that the other directors can give due weight to the opposing interest while assessing the director's views.

Articles frequently permit a director to hold any other office or place of profit under the company (other than the office of auditor) in conjunction with the office of director for such period and on such terms (as to remuneration and otherwise) as the directors may determine (see, for example, Table A, reg 84).[41] The articles usually go on to provide that, as long as disclosure of a director's interests has been made to the other directors, a director may be a party to or interested in any transaction or arrangement in which the company is interested, or may be associated with another body which is a party to a transaction or arrangement in which the company is interested (see, for example, Table A, reg 85(a) and (b)). An article in these terms will usually go

---

39 Persons connected with the director include the director's spouse, children and stepchildren under 18 years of age, the director's partner, companies with which the director is associated through control of one-fifth of the nominal equity capital or voting rights, and certain trustees.

40 The concept of 'shadow director' is defined in s 741(2) as 'a person in accordance with whose directions or instructions the directors of a company are accustomed to act', although those giving advice in a professional capacity are specifically excluded. For a recent case on the definition of 'shadow director' see *Re Hydrodan (Corby) Ltd* [1994] BCC 161.

41 Subject, however, to s 319 requiring the approval of a general meeting of any proposal to employ a director for more than five years when the contract is not freely terminable by the company during that period.

on to provide that a director so contracting or being so interested shall not be liable to account to the company for any profit realised by any such transactions or arrangement by reason of the director holding that office (for example, Table A, reg 85(c)).[42] In addition, the articles may permit a director, notwithstanding that director's interest, to be counted in the quorum present at any meeting at which that director or any other director is appointed to hold any such office or place of profit under the company or at which the terms of any such appointment are arranged, and allow a director to vote on any such appointment or arrangement other than his or her own appointment or the arrangement of the terms of that appointment. Finally, the articles may provide that a director may act, or his or her firm may act, in a professional capacity for the company, and that the director or the director's firm shall be entitled to remuneration for professional services as if that person were not a director. However, these provisions are stated not to authorise a director or a director's firm to act as auditor to the company. Many articles (particularly those of private companies) do not contain such an elaborate provision, but it is often useful to permit the restrictions imposed by the articles to be relaxed by the company in general meeting, especially where there are only two or three directors of the company.

It should be noted that all the provisions regarding disclosure and prohibitions on voting where there is an interest apply to a wider range of matters than merely 'contract'. Section 317 applies to contracts, transactions and arrangements. Regulations 84 and 85 apply to transactions and arrangements; and reg 94, barring directors from voting at a board meeting, does so in relation to matters in which they have an interest. These wide provisions re-enforce the director's fiduciary duty to disclose his or her interest in any matter which the board might consider, whether technically a contract with the company or not.

Committees

The directors may, if the articles contain the necessary authority, delegate their powers to a committee. The articles generally provide for this, as does Table A, reg 72. Where a company is regulated by an article in the form of reg 72, directors may delegate their powers to a committee of one.[43]

When a board of directors delegate their power to a committee without any provision as to the committee acting by a quorum, all acts of the committee must be done in the presence of all members of the committee, and the committee has no power to add to their number or to fill a vacancy.[44] The articles may, however, make provision for matters such as quorums for

---

42 This is subject, however, to the statutory rules on directors' contracts with the company. See note 38 above.

43 See, also, *Re Fireproof Doors* (1916) 2 Ch 142.

44 *Re Liverpool Household Stores* (1890) 59 LJ Ch 616.

committees. Table A, reg 72, for example, provides that subject to any conditions imposed by the board, the proceedings of a committee with two or more members shall be governed so far as possible by the rules in the articles regulating the proceedings of directors. A provision like this does not remove the need to ensure that, in all cases of delegation of powers to a committee, the committee's powers and authority are clearly stated in the resolution affecting the delegation.

Committees are usually appointed for one of three main purposes: first, to deal with a matter which requires speedy decision where the whole board could not be contacted quickly enough; secondly, to deal with a matter where it is desirable to have discussion free from the embarrassing presence of a director who is personally concerned in the matter, for example for the appointment or removal of a director to or from executive office (although the minutes, as distinct from a report on the discussions, are open to inspection by directors who were not on the committee, including the one being discussed); thirdly, for routine matters such as transfer, in which case standing committees are often appointed.

The power to delegate to a committee is, like all directors' powers, a fiduciary one. It cannot be exercised for an improper purpose, for example to exclude one or more directors from the forum where the board's decisions are taken.

CHAPTER 22

MEETINGS IN INSOLVENCY

Introduction

This Part has so far been concerned with meetings held in relation to the affairs of the company while it is a going concern and not directly threatened with proceedings in respect of insolvency. In this chapter, provisions dealing with the main meetings required to be held in connection with the insolvency of companies are noted. The central statutory provisions in this area are drawn from the Insolvency Act 1986 (IA 1986). The Insolvency Rules 1986, SI 1986/1925, also have an important role to play.[1]

Company voluntary arrangements

(1) Meetings to be held

The Act and the Rules make a distinction between company voluntary arrangements in two circumstances relevant to the issue of meetings. The first of these two circumstances is where the arrangement is proposed by the directors to the company and its creditors at a time when the company is not in administration and is not being wound up (IA 1986, s 1(1)). The second is where the proposal is made by the administrator or the liquidator (IA 1986, s 1(3)). There are some differences in the provisions relating to the required meetings in these two cases, which are explored below. There is also much common ground between the two types of company voluntary agreements. Both, for example, require a nominee who is a qualified insolvency practitioner in relation to the company to supervise the implementation of any arrangement agreed upon. Where the nominee is not the administrator or liquidator then meetings of members and creditors may be required if the nominee considers it necessary (IA 1986, s 2(2)). Where the nominee is the administrator or liquidator then meetings of members and creditors are obligatory (IA 1986, s 3(2)). The purpose of the meetings in both cases is to consider the proposals for the company voluntary arrangement and decide

---

1 References to Rules in this chapter will be to the Insolvency Rules 1986. For Scotland, reference should be made to the provisions governing procedure in Scotland and the Insolvency (Scotland) Rules 1986 (SI 1986/1915), as amended.

whether to agree to them, or to agree to them in some amended form. Neither meeting has an absolutely unfettered right to agree to any proposal (see the limitations in IA 1986, s 4(3) and (4) and s 6), but once held, the agreement of the meeting is essential for any proposal to go ahead.

(2) Notice

(a) *Nominee is not administrator or liquidator.* Where the nominee is not the administrator or liquidator, but has reported to the court under IA 1986, s 2(2) that the meetings should be held, then the nominee should, unless the court directs otherwise, summon the meetings for the time and place proposed in the report (IA 1986, s 3(1)). The date of the meeting should be not less than 14, nor more than 28 days after the filing of the report in the court (r 1.9(1)) and at least 14 days' notice should be given (r 1.9(2)).

So far as the creditors' meeting is concerned, notice must be given to all creditors, the name and address of whom the nominee is aware (IA 1986, s 3(3); see also r 1.9(2)(a)). So far as the members' meeting is concerned, notice must be sent to all persons who are, according to the nominee's belief, members (r 1.9(2)(b)). Fourteen days' notice of both meetings should also be given to the directors and officers and any person who the convenor considers should be present because that person was a director or officer of the company during the two years immediately preceding the notice (r 1.16(1)).

For both creditors' and members' meetings the notice should, of course, stipulate the time and place of the meeting. The time of the meeting must be fixed for between 10.00 am and 4.00 pm on a business day (r 1.13(2)), and although both the members' and creditors' meetings should be held on the same day and at the same place, the creditors' meeting must be held before the members' meeting (r 1.13(3)). This reflection of the status accorded to creditors in a company voluntary arrangement is also shown by the fact that in fixing the venue, the convenience of the creditors should be accorded primary regard (r 1.13(1)).

Certain other matters are also required to be stated in the notice. These are laid down in r 1.9(3) and include a specification of the court to which the nominee's report has been delivered; a statement of the rules on requisite majorities; a copy of the proposal; a copy or summary of the statement of affairs; and the nominee's comments on the proposal. The notice must also be accompanied by a proxy form (r 1.13(4)).

(b) *Nominee is administrator or liquidator.* Where the nominee is the administrator or liquidator then the nominee should summon the meeting for the time and place he or she thinks fit (IA 1986, s 3(3)). At least 14 days' notice must be given of the meetings (r 1.11(1)). The creditors, members, directors, officers, former directors and former officers to whom notice should be sent are the same as those identified above in relation to a company voluntary agreement where the company is not in administration or liquidation (see IA 1986, s 3(3) and r 1.11). The provisions on the fixing of time and place of the meeting are also the same (r 1.13). In addition to stating the time and place of the relevant meeting, the notice must also state the effect of the rules on requisite majorities, include a copy of the insolvency practitioner's proposal, and include a copy or summary of the statement of affairs (r 1.11(2)). The notice must be accompanied by a proxy form (r 1.13(4)).

(3) Chairman

The convenor of the meeting is also to be the chairman of the meeting (r 1.14(1)). If, however, the convenor is for some reason unable to attend the meeting, the convenor may nominate as chairman a person qualified as an insolvency practitioner in relation to the company, or an employee of the convenor or the convenor's firm experienced in insolvency matters. The Rules lay down a number of powers to be enjoyed by the chairman in addition to the chairman's usual power to regulate the meeting. The chairman may exclude any director, officer, former director or former officer from attending all or part of a meeting, even where that person has been sent a notice of the meeting (r 1.16(2)). The chairman also has a discretion to reject the whole or part of a creditor's claim to be entitled to vote (r 1.17(4)), although if the chairman is in doubt as to the validity of the claim he or she may mark the claim as objected to but allow the creditor to vote (r 1.17(6)). The decision of a chairman to reject the claim to vote of a creditor is subject to appeal to the court by a member or creditor (r 1.17(5)), but any appeal must be made within 28 days from the day that the report on the meetings under IA 1986, s 4(6) has been made to the court (r 1.17(8)). Particular powers of the chairman in relation to creditors' meetings are conferred by r 1.19(5). This sub-rule confers on the chairman power to decide whether creditors' votes ought to be left out of account because they are secured in some way, and also power to decide whose votes should be discounted on the basis that they are a connected person (these matters are discussed further below). These powers conferred by r 1.19(5) should be exercised by the chairman in reliance upon the company's statement of affairs.

There is a limitation on the chairman's power when exercising proxy votes. Essentially, unless specifically directed to do so by the appointor, the chairman cannot use proxies to change the amount of remuneration and expenses of the nominee or any supervisor of the proposed arrangement (r 1.15).

(4) Adjournment

The provisions on adjournment of the meetings convened for the purpose of approving a company voluntary arrangement are contained in r 1.21. Not only does the chairman have power to adjourn the meetings, but if the chairman thinks fit, he or she may procure the holding of the creditors' and members' meeting together (r 1.21(1)). Neither the creditors' meeting nor the members' meeting may be adjourned unless the other is also adjourned to the same business day (r 1.21(4)).

The chairman's power of adjournment may only be exercised for the purpose of achieving the requisite majority for the approval of the proposed arrangement (r 1.21(2)). However, even where the meetings are adjourned several times, the final meetings must take place within 14 days of the day originally set down for the holding of the meetings (r 1.21(3)).

The chairman's power to adjourn may be exercised without a resolution of the meeting, but where such a resolution is passed the chairman must adjourn the meeting (r 1.21(2)). Where the proposal for the company voluntary arrangement has been made by the directors and the meeting has been adjourned the nominee must immediately give notice of that fact to the court (r 1.21(5)).

(5) Voting

(a) *Creditors' meeting.* Every creditor given notice of the meeting is entitled to vote (r 1.17(1)). The calculation of a creditor's voting power is made according to the quantum of the creditor's debt at the date of the meeting, or, where the company is in administration or liquidation, at the date of the administration or liquidation order (r 1.17(2)). Unless the chairman agrees to an estimated value, there is no right to vote in respect of an unliquidated debt or a debt for an unascertained amount (r 1.17(3)). Certain parts of debt for an ascertained amount are also to be discounted in the voting process. The discounted interests are laid down in r 1.19(3), which basically excludes amounts of the debt which are in any way secured and debts in respect of which written notice has not been given to the chairman.

The required majority in the creditors' meeting for approval or modification of the proposed arrangement is three-quarters by value (r 1.19(1)). For any other resolution the required majority is one half (r 1.19(2)). However, these required majorities are subject to the rule that any resolution will be invalid if half of the value of valid votes are cast against it, unless that half includes persons connected with the company (r 1.19(4)).

The proposal is deemed to have been rejected if both the creditors' and members' meetings fail to approve it, or a modified version of it, at or before a final adjourned meeting (r 1.21(6)).

(b) *Members' meeting.* Calculation of members' voting rights is considerably more straightforward than those of creditors. Members' voting rights are simply as defined in the articles (r 1.18(1)). This is subject to one qualification, which is that members with no voting rights under the articles may vote (r 1.18(2)). The exercise of such a vote, however, seems largely symbolic. This is because such votes are discounted when calculating the requisite majority, which is one half in value of the members unless the articles otherwise provide (r 1.20).

As stated above, the proposal is deemed to have been rejected if the creditors' meeting and the members' meeting fail to approve it at or before the final adjourned meetings (r 1.21(6)).

(6) Report

Section 4(6) of IA 1986 requires the chairman to report the result of the meeting to the court within four days of the holding of the meeting (r 1.24(3)). The report must contain a statement on the fate of the proposals; set out each of the resolutions taken at the meeting and the decisions on each; list those present or represented at the meeting, the value of their votes and how they voted on the resolutions; and any other information of which the chairman thinks the court should be aware (r 1.24(2)). Where a voluntary arrangement has been approved, a copy of this report must also be sent to the registrar (r 1.24(5)).

Notice of the results of the meeting should be sent to all persons who received notice of the meeting (r 1.24(4)).

Company administration

(1) Creditors' meeting

Section 23(1)(b), IA 1986 requires an administrator to place a statement of his or her proposals for achieving the purposes specified in the administration order before a meeting of the company's creditors within three months of the making of the administration order. The meeting is required to consider whether or not to approve the administrator's proposals (IA 1986, s 24(1)) and is entitled to approve the proposals with modifications providing the administrator consents to the modifications (IA 1986, s 24(2)).

(2) Notice

Section 23(1)(b), IA 1986 provides for at least 14 days' notice of the meeting. Rule 2.18 requires notice to be given to all creditors and to all directors and officers who the administrator considers ought to be present at the meeting. A proxy form should accompany the notice (r 2.19(5)). Notice of the meeting should also be advertised in the same newspaper in which the administration was advertised.

Unless the court otherwise directs, the meeting should be convened for a business day between the hours of 10.00 am and 4.00 pm (r 2.19(3)); and the venue should be fixed with respect to the convenience of the creditors (r 2.19(2)).

(3) Identity of creditors

The creditors required to be summoned to the meeting are all creditors identified in the statement of affairs and all other creditors known to the administrator who had outstanding claims against the company at the date of the administration order (r 2.18(1)). The identity of those creditors entitled to vote at the meeting is discussed below.

(4) Chairman

The chairman at a meeting of this type must be the administrator or any person nominated by the administrator provided they are eligible to act as chairman. Eligible persons are either qualified insolvency practitioners in relation to the particular company, or employees of the administrator or the administrator's firm experienced in the handling of such matters (r 2.20).

   As is the case with any company meeting, the chairman has considerable power with respect to the proceedings. In particular, with respect to creditors' meetings in an administration, the chairman may admit or reject the whole or part of a creditor's claim to vote (r 2.23(1)). If, however, the chairman is in any doubt about whether a creditor has a right to vote or not, then the chairman ought to mark the claim as objected to but nevertheless allow the creditor in question to vote (r 2.23(3)). Any challenge in court to the chairman's exercise of these powers must be made within 14 days from the delivery by the administrator of the report on the outcome of the meeting to the court, which is required under IA 1986, s 24(4).

   It is the chairman's duty to see that minutes of the proceedings at the meeting are entered into the company's minute-book (r 2.28(2)). The minutes must include a list of creditors who attended personally or by proxy and, if a creditors' committee has been established, the names and addresses of its members (r 2.28(3)).

(5) Adjournment

The Rules lay down three circumstances in which the meeting may be adjourned. First, the chairman may, and if a resolution is passed to that effect shall, adjourn the meeting if there is not the requisite majority approving the administrator's proposals. (The requisite majority is discussed below.) The meeting cannot be adjourned for more than 14 days on this ground (r 2.18(4)). Secondly, if there is no chairman within 30 minutes of the time set down for the commencement of the meeting then the meeting is adjourned to the same time and place in the following week. If the new time falls on a day which is not a business day (because, for example, it is a Bank Holiday), then the meeting is adjourned to the business day immediately following (r 2.19(6)). Thirdly, the chairman may exercise his or her discretion to adjourn the meeting for a period not exceeding 14 days (r 2.19(7)).

(6) Voting

The persons entitled to vote at a creditor's meeting of a company in administration are those creditors who have given the administrator details of the debt which is allegedly due from the company before noon on the business day before the meeting and which have had that debt approved (in accordance with r 2.22) and, where the creditor intends to vote by proxy, have lodged with the administrator the proxy intended to be used (r 2.22(1)). The chairman does, however, have a discretion to permit a person to vote even where they have failed to comply with these requirements (r 2.22(2)).

Rule 2.22(1) requires that the details of the debt to be given to the administrator must include any calculation required under rr 2.24 to 2.27. As votes are calculated against the amounts of the creditor's debt (r 2.22(4)), these calculations are relevant to computing the voting power of each creditor. The calculations in rr 2.24 to 2.27 relate respectively to: secured creditors; holders of negotiable instruments; retention of title creditors; and hire purchase, conditional sale and chattel leasing agreements. In very general terms, they require creditors holding these types of interests to make an allowance in respect of the security which they hold. This allowance is deducted from the creditor's debt for the purpose of calculation of the creditor's vote.

The majority required is a simple one (r 2.28(1)), but a resolution will not be valid where more than half in value of the creditors vote against it provided that those creditors making up the half against the resolution are not, to the chairman's knowledge, persons connected with the company (r 2.28(1A)). Application of these rules may require a relatively time-consuming calculation, especially since creditors are entitled to split their vote on the basis of value and vote a certain amount of value one way and a certain amount another.[2]

(7) Administrator's report

After the meeting the administrator must report the result of the meeting to the court (IA 1986, s 24(4)). Details of the proposals and any revisions or modifications to the proposals considered at the meeting should be annexed to the report (r 2.29). The report should also be sent to creditors (see r 2.30).

(8) Creditors' committee

The creditors' meeting may establish a creditors' committee (IA 1986, s 49). Rules 2.34 to 2.45 govern the meetings of such committees.

---

2 *Re Polly Peck International plc* [1991] BCC 503.

Administrative receivership

(1) Creditors' meeting

Within three months of the appointment of an administrative receiver, he or she must make a report in accordance with IA 1986, s 48(1) which must be sent to the Registrar, trustees for secured creditors, secured creditors and unsecured creditors. The obligation to send the report to the unsecured creditors can also be discharged by publishing a notice stating an address to which unsecured creditors may write in order to receive a copy of the report free of charge (IA 1986, s 48(2)). The administrative receiver is then required, unless the court otherwise directs, to lay a copy of the report before a meeting of the unsecured creditors (s 48(2)). The court may only give a direction to the contrary if the administrative receiver's report states an intention to apply for such a direction and a copy of the report has been sent to all unsecured creditors (or a notice has been published inviting them to send for the report) at least 14 days before the hearing of the application for a direction. The only circumstance in which a meeting of unsecured creditors can be dispensed with without a direction from the court is where the company has gone into liquidation and the administrative receiver complies with the requirements of IA 1986, s 48(4).

(2) Notice

At least 14 days' notice of the meeting must be given to all creditors identified in the statement of affairs and to any other creditors that the administrative receiver knows had a claim against the company at the date of his or her appointment (IA 1986, s 48(2); r 3.9(3)). The notice should also be published in the same newspaper in which the receiver's appointment was advertised (r 3.9(6)).

The notice must, of course, give the time and place of the meeting. The place of the meeting must be fixed having regard to the convenience of those entitled to attend (r 3.9(1)) and it must be held between 10.00 am and 4.00 pm on a business day (r 3.9(2)). In addition to stating time and place, the notice must also state: first, that creditors whose entire claim against the company is secured may not attend or be represented at the meeting (r 3.9(5)); and secondly, the effect of the provisions on voting rights in r 3.11(1) (r 3.9(11)). The notice must be accompanied by a proxy form (r 3.9(4)).

(3) Creditors entitled to participate in the meeting

As already noted, the meeting is a meeting of unsecured creditors. This means that secured creditors may only vote in respect of the balance of the debt due after deducting the value of the security held (r 3.11(6)). So far as creditors whose debt is secured by a bill of exchange or a promissory note are concerned, they may only vote if they are willing to treat the liability of every person liable antecedently to the company as security, or if they are prepared to estimate the value of the security and deduct it from their claim against the company for the purpose of calculating voting rights (r 3.11(7)).

No creditor qualified to vote may vote at the meeting unless they have given the administrative receiver details of the debt claimed to be due by 12 noon on the business day before the meeting and the claim has been admitted under r 3.11 (r. 3.11(1)(a)). Where a creditor wishes to vote by proxy, the proxy must be lodged with the administrative receiver (r 3.11(1)(b)).

(4) Chairman

The chairman at the meeting is the administrative receiver or a person nominated by the administrative receiver (r 3.10(1)). The administrative receiver may only nominate another person to be the chairman if that person is a qualified insolvency practitioner in relation to the company, or an employee of the receiver or the receiver's firm who is experienced in insolvency matters (r 3.10(2)).

The Rules confer on the chairman a number of specific powers in addition to the chairman's usual powers to regulate the meeting. Most of the additional powers relate to qualification for voting. The chairman has, for instance, a discretion to allow a creditor who has failed to submit details in writing of the debt due from the company before 12 noon on the business day preceding the meeting to vote notwithstanding this omission (r 3.11(2)). The chairman may also call for the production of documents or evidence to support a creditor's claim (r 3.11(3)). The chairman may, whether he or she has called for the production of documents or other evidence or not, reject the whole or part of a creditor's entitlement to vote (r 3.12(1)); or, if unsure about the admissibility of a claim to be entitled to vote, mark it as objected to but allow it to proceed in the first instance (r 3.12(3)). The chairman's decision on entitlement to vote is subject to an appeal by any creditor to the court (r 3.12(2)) and if the chairman's decision is varied on appeal the court may summon another meeting or make any such order as it considers just (r 3.12(4); (see also r 3.12(5) as to costs of the appeal). Finally, the chairman is charged with the duty of ensuring that a record of the proceedings is made (r 3.15(2)). The record must show the names of the creditors attending in person or by proxy and, if a committee of creditors is appointed, the names and addresses of its members (r 3.15(3)).

(5) Adjournment

The power of adjournment resides solely in the chairman, who may adjourn the meeting to such time and place as he or she thinks fit (r 3.14(1)).

(6) Voting

As with the other types of creditors' meetings considered earlier, the vote is calculated by reference to the unsecured amount owing to the creditor (r 3.11(4)). Any amounts paid in respect of the debt since the appointment of the receiver should be deducted when making this calculation (r 3.11(4)). Since the size of the debt is relevant to making the calculation on voting power, a vote may not be cast in respect of an unliquidated or unascertained debt, unless the chairman agrees to an estimated minimum value for the purpose of calculating the voting power of a creditor holding such a debt (r 3.11(5)). This power to estimate a minimum value is also subject to appeal to the court under r 3.12(2), see above.

The required majority for passing a resolution at this type of creditors' meeting is a simple majority in value of those voting (r 3.15(1)).

(7) Creditors' committee

One of the things which the creditors' meeting in an administrative receivership may do is to establish a creditors' committee to assist the administrative receiver in the discharge of his or her functions (IA 1986, s 49 and r 3.18(1)). The proceedings at meetings of such a committee are governed by rr 3.18 to 3.30A.

Members' voluntary winding up

A voluntary winding up may be either a members' voluntary winding up or a creditors' voluntary winding up. It will be a members' voluntary winding up where the directors have made a statutory declaration of solvency in accordance with IA 1986, s 89 (IA 1986, s 90).

A number of company meetings are required in order to effect a members' voluntary winding up. First, there must be a meeting in which it is resolved to wind the company up. This meeting must pass an ordinary resolution that the company be wound up where the duration of the company as fixed by the articles expires or an event occurs on the occurrence of which the articles provide that the company is to be dissolved (IA 1986, s 84(1)(a)); a special resolution that the company be wound up voluntarily (s 84(1)(b)) or an extraordinary resolution to the effect that winding up is advisable due to the fact that the company's liabilities prevent it continuing its business (s 84(1)(c)). Secondly, the company must hold a meeting to appoint liquidators (IA 1986, s 91(1)) and, if necessary, to fill any vacancy in the position of liquidator (IA 1986, s 92(1)). Thirdly, if the winding up process lasts for more than a year the liquidator must summon a general meeting of the company at the end of the first year from the commencement of the winding up and each succeeding year (IA 1986, s 93(1)) so that the liquidator can lay before the meeting an account of his or her handling of the winding up (IA 1986, s 93(2)). Finally, once the company's affairs are fully wound up the liquidator must call a final meeting and lay before it an account of the winding up of the company's affairs (IA 1986, s 94(1)).

Subject to the qualifications noted here, these meetings are held in accordance with the usual procedures and conduct for company meetings. So far as the initial meeting is concerned, an additional obligation is the requirement that notice of the resolution be given in the *Gazette* within 14 days of its passing (IA 1986, s 85); also, in order for the winding up to be a members' voluntary winding up, the directors' statutory declaration of solvency must be made within the five weeks immediately preceding the passing of the resolution (IA 1986, s 89(2)(a)).

No special requirements are made in respect of the meeting to appoint the liquidator, although it should be noted that once appointed the liquidator comes under an obligation to publicise and give notice to certain parties of his or her appointment (see r 4.106). This also applies to any liquidator appointed to fill a casual vacancy. Where a meeting has to be held to fill such a casual vacancy, this must be convened by a contributory (the concept of 'contributory' is discussed below) or by any continuing liquidators (IA 1986, s 92(2)). The reason for this is that at the time of the initial appointment of a liquidator the directors' powers generally cease (IA 1986, s 91(2)). Aside from the special arrangements for convening a meeting to fill a casual vacancy in the office of liquidator, such a meeting is held in the usual manner unless otherwise determined by the court (IA 1986, s 92(3)).

As has already been noted, any general meetings called where the winding up lasts for more than one year, and also the final meeting prior to dissolution, must be convened by the liquidator. Again, this is a consequence of the cessation of the directors' powers. Certain other deviations from the normal procedure are also prescribed in respect of the final meeting prior to dissolution. First, the meeting is to be called by an advertisement in the *Gazette*, published at least a month before the meeting, specifying its time, place and object (IA 1986, s 94(2)). Secondly, within a week of holding the meeting, the liquidator must make a return to the Registrar specifying that the meeting is taking place on a certain date and must send the Registrar a copy of the account laid before the final meeting (IA 1986, s 94(3) and see the Insolvency Rules, Form 4.71 as to the form of the return). If the final meeting is inquorate then the liquidator's return should note that the meeting was duly summoned but was inquorate (IA 1986, 94(5)). The filing of the final account and return with the Registrar starts the process of dissolution of the company which, in the ordinary case, is deemed to have occurred within three months of the filing (IA 1986, s 201(2), but note the power of the court in s 201(3) and (4) to defer the date of dissolution).

Creditors' voluntary winding up

(1) Meetings to be held

As already noted, a voluntary winding up will be a creditors' voluntary winding up where the directors have not made a declaration of solvency in accordance with IA 1986, s 89 (IA 1986, s 90). There is also provision for a members' voluntary winding up to be converted to a creditors' voluntary winding up (IA 1986, s 96).

The same types of meetings are required in a creditors' voluntary winding up as for a members' voluntary winding up with the added complication that separate creditors' meetings are required for all the types of meetings listed in relation to members' voluntary winding up except the initial meeting of the company at which the resolution to wind up is passed. In a creditors' voluntary winding up, once the initial resolution has been passed by the company, the next meeting required is a meeting of creditors (IA 1986, s 98) at which the directors must lay a statement of affairs before the creditors in accordance with IA 1986, s 99. This first meeting of creditors may also appoint a liquidator (IA 1986, s 100; see s 100(3) with respect to the situation where the creditors' and the members' meeting nominate different liquidators) and a liquidation committee (IA 1986, s 101). (See, further, r 4.53 as to the business of the first meeting of creditors.) The creditors may also fill any casual vacancy in the office of liquidator (IA 1986, s 104). If the winding up has been converted from a members' voluntary winding up to a creditors' voluntary winding up then the first creditors' meeting does not need to be held as its function will already have been satisfied by the creditors' meeting held in accordance with IA 1986, s 95, which is necessary for the conversion to a creditors' voluntary winding up (IA 1986, s 96). The other meetings which must be held in a creditors' voluntary winding up are creditors' and members' meetings held annually where the winding up lasts more than a year, and final creditors' and members' meetings prior to dissolution. The liquidator may also, at any time, summon meetings of creditors and contributories in order to ascertain their wishes (see r 4.54). Similarly, creditors may requisition meetings (see r 4.57). The procedure for the holding of all the members' meetings in a creditors' voluntary winding up is the same as that discussed above in relation to a members' voluntary winding up. The creditors' meetings are, however, subject to special provisions in both the Insolvency Act 1986 and the Insolvency Rules.

(2) Creditors' meetings: notice

The first meeting of creditors under IA 1986, s 98 must be summoned by the company within 14 days from the day upon which the resolution for winding up is to be proposed (IA 1986, s 98(1)(a)). Unless the court makes an order under r 4.59 that the notice of the meeting is to be given by public advertisement rather than individually, the notice must be sent to the creditors by post at least seven days before the day on which the meeting is to be held (IA 1986, s 98(1)(b)) and the notice must be advertised in the *Gazette* and in at least two newspapers circulating in the locality of the company's principal place of business (IA 1986, s 98(1)(c); see IA 1986, s 98(3) and (4) where the company has more than one principal place of business or the principal place of business is not in the UK). Past and present officers may also be summoned to attend the meeting in accordance with r 4.58.

The notice must specify the time and place of the meeting and the place where proxies are to be lodged (r 4.51(2)). Reading together r 4.51(2) and r 4.60(2), it appears that the first meeting of creditors must be held between 12 noon and 4.00 pm on a business day. The venue must be fixed with regard to the convenience of the creditors (r 4.60(1)). The notice must also state one of the following: the name of a qualified insolvency practitioner who will furnish the creditors free of charge with any information they reasonably require about the company's affairs; or an address at which, during the two days preceding the date for the meeting, a list of the names and addresses of the company creditors will be available free of charge (IA 1986, s 98(2)). The notice must be accompanied by a proxy form (r 4.60(3)).

Annual meetings of creditors must be summoned by the liquidator within three months of the end of the year in question (IA 1986, s 105(1)). Twenty-one days' notice specifying the purpose of the meeting (r 4.54(3)) must be given to all creditors known to the liquidator or identified in the company's statement of affairs (r 4.54(2)(a)), although the court may order the notice of meetings to be by public advertisement only (r 4.59). The liquidator may also summon company personnel (r 4.58(2)). The place of the meeting must be fixed having regard to the convenience of the creditors (r 4.60(1)) and it must be held between 10.00 am and 4.00 pm on a business day (r 4.60(2)). In addition to stating these matters, the notice must also state a time and place not more than four days before the meeting for the lodging of proxies (r 4.54(5)). A proxy form must accompany the notice (r 4.60(3)).

At least 28 days' notice of the final meeting before dissolution must be given to all creditors who have proved their debts (r 4.126(1)). An advertisement stating the time, place and object of the meeting must also be published in the *Gazette* at least one month before the meeting (IA 1986, s 106(2)). Otherwise the rules on notice for this meeting are the same as for the annual creditors' meetings.

(3) Creditors' meetings: chairman

Except at the first meetings of creditors, the chairman at meetings of creditors in a creditors' voluntary winding up should be the liquidator or a person nominated by the liquidator (r 4.56). A person nominated by the liquidator must be a qualified insolvency practitioner in relation to the company, or an employee of the liquidator or the liquidator's firm with experience in insolvency matters (r 4.56(2)). At the first meeting of creditors, the

chairman must be a director appointed by the other directors for that purpose
(IA 1986, s 99(1)).

The rules confer specific powers and duties on the chairman of a creditors'
meeting. The chairman has a discretion in relation to the admission to the
meeting of company personnel (r 4.58(5)); certain discretions in relation to
adjournment, which are discussed below; a discretion in relation to admitting
the votes of creditors who have failed to satisfy the rules on lodging proofs
where the chairman believes that the failure was beyond the creditor's control
(r 4.68); discretion to admit or reject any creditors' proof with respect to
entitlement to vote (r 4.70(1)) or to mark a proof as objected to in the usual
way (r 4.70(3)). The chairman's decisions on entitlement to vote may be
appealed to the court by any creditor or contributory (r 4.70(2)).

Where the chairman holds a proxy instructing the chairman to vote for a
particular resolution and that resolution is not proposed by anyone else, then
the chairman is required to propose it unless there is a good reason, in the
chairman's view, for not doing so (r 4.64(a)). If the chairman does not
propose a resolution in these circumstances, he or she must notify the
appointor of the proxy of the reason for this immediately after the meeting
(r 4.64(b)).

The other specific duties imposed on the chairman are keeping minutes as
part of the record of the liquidation (r 4.71(1)), and keeping a list of all
creditors attending the meeting (r 4.71(2)).

(4) Creditors' meetings: adjournment and suspension

The chairman of a creditors' meeting has power not only to adjourn the
meeting in his or her discretion (r 4.65(3) and (4)), but also, during the course
of the meeting, to suspend it once for up to one hour (r 4.65(2)). The
chairman must adjourn the meeting if the meeting so resolves (r 4.65(3)). The
adjourned meeting will be held at such time or place as the chairman deter-
mines (r 4.65(3) and (4)). However, this discretion is qualified to the extent
that the adjournment may not be for more than 21 days and the usual rules
(r 4.60(1) and (2)) as to fixing the time and place of meetings apply
(r 4.65(5)). The meeting will also be adjourned where there is no chairman
present and none is agreed upon (r 4.65(6)). In this case, the adjournment will
be to the same time and place in the following week, unless that falls on a day
which is not a business day, in which case the meeting will be adjourned to the
next business day following that day (r 4.65(6)). Where the meeting has been
adjourned, proofs and proxies may be lodged any time before midday on the
business day before the adjourned meeting (r 4.65(7)). Except where the
meeting has been adjourned because there is no chairman, the chairman
should give notice of adjournments to any of the company's personnel, not
present at the meeting, as he or she thinks appropriate (r 4.58(3)).

Finally, it should be noted that a special provision is made with respect to the
circumstances where the meeting of the company at which the resolution to

wind up is to be proposed under IA 1986, s 84 is adjourned and the first meeting of creditors takes place before it. Where this happens then any resolution passed at the first meeting of creditors will not take effect until the company passes a resolution to wind up (r 4.53A).

(5) Creditors' meeting: voting

A person is only entitled to vote at a creditors' meeting in a creditors' voluntary winding up if they have lodged a proof of debt and the claim to vote has been admitted by the chairman under r 4.70(1) (r 4.67(1)(a)). If a creditor wishes to vote by proxy they must also lodge the proxy as required in the notice for the meeting (r 4.67(1)(b)). The chairman's power to allow a creditor to vote without proving their debt (r 4.68) has been noted above. The court also has the power in exceptional circumstances to allow creditors, or a class of creditors, to vote without proving their debts (r 4.67(2)).

As in other types of creditors' meetings considered in this chapter, voting power is calculated by reference to the value of the debt owed (r 4.63(1)). Similarly, for the purpose of calculating voting rights, deductions must be made in respect of any type of security (r 4.67(4) and (5)(b)) or the holders of bills of exchange and promissory notes must treat the liability of those antecedent to the company as security (r 4.67(5)(a)), and an estimated minimum amount must be placed upon unliquidated or unascertained debts (r 4.67(3)).

The required majority is a simple majority in value of those voting (r 4.63(1)), although on any resolution affecting the office of liquidator the vote of the liquidator or any partner or employee of the liquidator cannot be counted as part of the majority (r 4.63(4)).

(6) Return to Registrar on final meetings prior to dissolution

In a creditors' voluntary winding up the liquidator must send a copy of the account of the liquidation which has been laid before the final members' meeting and the final creditors' meeting and a return concerning both meetings to the Registrar (see Insolvency Rules, Form 4.72) in the same way as required in respect of the final members' meeting in a members' voluntary winding up, as discussed above (IA 1986, s 106). As in a members' voluntary winding up, this triggers the dissolution of the company which will occur within three months of the filing (IA 1986, s 201(2)), subject to the court's power to defer the date of dissolution (s 201(3) and (4)).

Winding up by the court

(1) Meetings to be held

The circumstances in which a company may be wound up by the court are contained in IA 1986, s 122. One of those circumstances is that the company has resolved by special resolution to that effect (s 122(1)(a)). Where this is relevant, the special resolution should be passed in the same manner as any other special resolution of the company. Six other possible circumstances leading to a winding up by the court are also listed; thus, in many cases it is not unlikely that there will be no initial meeting of the company to pass a special resolution for winding up by the court.

Once winding up by the court has commenced, the official receiver must decide within 12 weeks, beginning on the day the winding up order was made, whether or not to exercise the power under IA 1986, s 136(4) to summon separate meetings of creditors and contributories for the purpose of choosing someone other than the official receiver to be the liquidator (s 136(5)(a)). The official receiver is required to exercise the power to call such meetings when requested to by one-quarter in value of the company's creditors. The choice of the liquidator at such meetings of creditors and contributories is governed by IA 1986, s 139. Such meetings may also appoint a liquidation committee (IA 1986, s 141; see, further, r 4.52 as to the business of such meetings). Meetings summoned by the official receiver under the power in IA 1986, s 136(4) are referred to in the Rules (and in this part of this chapter), respectively, as 'the first meeting of creditors' and 'the first meeting of contributories' and together as 'the first meetings in liquidation' (r 4.50(7)).

Where the liquidator is not the official receiver, a final meeting of creditors must be summoned by the liquidator at which the liquidator's report on the winding up should be presented and the meeting should determine whether to release the liquidator (IA 1986, s 146(1)). As in a creditors' voluntary winding up, the official receiver or the liquidator also has the power to call meetings of creditors or of contributories in order to ascertain their wishes (r 4.54); and the creditors or contributories may also requisition a meeting (r 4.57). As will be seen, these are only some of a number of similarities in the rules on meetings of creditors in a creditors' voluntary winding up and meetings of creditors or contributories in a winding up by the court. The discussion below seeks to highlight the differences rather than repeating provisions in the rules common to both types of winding up.

(2) Contributories

A contributory is any person liable to contribute to the company in the event of its winding up (IA 1986, s 79).

(3) Notice

Where the official receiver decides to exercise the power to call first meetings of creditors and contributories, he or she must fix venues for each meeting within four months of the winding-up order (r 4.50(1)). Where the official receiver is required by the creditors to call first meetings under IA 1986, s 136(5)(c), he or she must fix a venue within three months of the receipt of the request (r 4.50(6)(b)). At least 21 days' notice of each meeting must be given to the court and, respectively, to every creditor known to the official receiver or identified in the statement of affairs, and to every person appearing in the company's books or otherwise as a contributory (r 4.50 (2)). The notices must specify the usual matters regarding time and place, as discussed above (r 4.60(1) and (2)) and must be accompanied by a proxy form (r 4.60(3)). Additionally, the notice must specify a time not more than four days before the meeting for the lodgement of, in the case of a creditors' meeting, proofs and proxies and, in the case of a contributories' meeting, proxies (r 4.50(4)). Notice of the meetings must also be publicly advertised (r 4.50(5)).

For the final meeting of creditors at least 28 days' notice must be given to all creditors who have proved their debts and the notice should also appear in the *Gazette* at least one month before the meeting (r 4.125(1); and see Insolvency Rules, Form 4.22).

(4) Chairman

Where a meeting in a winding up by the court is convened by the official receiver, as will be the case for the first meetings in liquidation, then the official receiver or a person nominated in writing by the official receiver is the chairman (r 4.55(2)). A written nomination is not necessary, however, where the person nominated is another official receiver or a deputy official receiver. Where the convenor is not the official receiver, as will be the case for the final meeting summoned by the liquidator under IA 1986, s 146, then the convenor or a person nominated in writing by the convenor is the chairman (r 4.55(3)). However, where the convenor is not the official receiver, the convenor may only nominate another person as chairman if that person is a qualified insolvency practitioner in relation to the company or an employee of the liquidator or the liquidator's firm experienced in insolvency matters (r 4.55(3)).

The powers and duties of the chairman in creditors' and contributories' meetings in a winding up by the court are the same as those in a creditors' voluntary winding up (as discussed above), except for the following two matters. First, in a winding up by the court the chairman does not have a discretion to allow a creditor to vote notwithstanding the creditor's failure to comply with the rules on lodging proofs of debt by a certain time, although the chairman still has the same power to admit or reject a proof for the purpose of entitlement to vote (r 4.70(1)). Secondly, in a winding up by the court the chairman must not only make a record of resolutions passed (r 4.71(3)), he or she must also file certified particulars of such resolutions in court within 21 days of the meeting (r 4.71(4)).

(5) Adjournment

The rules on adjournment are the same for creditors' and contributories' meetings in a winding up by the court as they are for creditors' meetings in a creditors' voluntary winding up.

(6) Voting

Subject to the absence of the chairman's discretion to allow a creditor to vote where the creditor has failed to lodge a proof by the due date (as discussed above), the rules on voting are the same for creditors' and contributories' meetings in a winding up by the court as they are for creditors' meetings in a creditors' voluntary winding up.

(7) Report to the court

After the final meeting of creditors required under IA 1986, s 146 has been held, the liquidator must give notice to the court of the holding of the meeting (see Insolvency Rules, Form 4.42) and a copy of the report must be sent to the official receiver. The notice must state whether or not the meeting has resolved to release the liquidator and must be accompanied by a copy of the report laid before the final meeting by the liquidator (r 4.125(4)). This report must give an account of the winding up including, in particular, a summary of receipts and payments and a statement by the liquidator that the account given has been reconciled with that held by the Secretary of State with respect to the winding up (r 4.125(2)). If the final meeting is inquorate, the liquidator must report this fact to the court, in which case the meeting is deemed to have been held and the liquidator deemed released (r 4.125(5)).

MEETINGS OF LOCAL AUTHORITIES

CHAPTER 23

MEETINGS OF LOCAL AUTHORITIES

Introduction

The Local Government Act 1972 reorganised local government in England and Wales (excluding Greater London, the local government of which was reorganised by the London Government Act 1963). The Local Government Act 1985 further reformed the structure of local government. In outline, the structure of local government is as follows:

(a) Under the Local Government Act 1972, England and Wales were divided into 53 counties (6 are metropolitan counties) and 369 districts (36 are metropolitan districts). The London Government Act 1963 had established the Greater London Council and 32 London borough councils to undertake local government functions in Greater London. All counties and districts, including London boroughs, have councils, which are known as principal councils. The Local Government Act 1985 abolished the Greater London Council and metropolitan county councils and transferred their functions to other bodies, principally to the London borough councils, metropolitan district councils and to joint authorities established to undertake particular functions which were previously carried out by the Greater London Council and metropolitan county councils.

(b) Below the level of principal councils, there is a distinction between England and Wales:

    (i) In some parts of England, some districts are subdivided into parishes. Every parish has a parish meeting, and some parishes have a parish council.

    (ii) In Wales, all districts are subdivided into communities. Every community has a community meeting, and some communities have a community council.

Meetings

There are three sources of rules governing the meetings of local authorities, parish and community meetings.

(1) Statute

The main statutory provisions relating to the meetings of local authorities, parish and community meetings are set out in Parts I–VI of the Twelfth Schedule to the Local Government Act 1972. Part I of the Twelfth Schedule relates to the meetings of principal councils, and Part IA (inserted by the Local Government Act 1985, Sch 14, para 35) applies the provisions of Part I, subject to minor modifications to the meetings of joint authorities. Part II relates to parish councils, Part III to parish meetings, Part IV to community councils and Part V to community meetings. Part VI of the Twelfth Schedule contains provisions relating to the meetings of local authorities generally.

(2) Standing orders

An authority can make standing orders provided these are not inconsistent with the statutory provisions to govern its meetings.

(3) General principles

Where a matter is not covered by the statutory provisions or standing orders, then the general principles governing meetings discussed in Part I apply.

Annual meetings

(1) Principal councils, joint authorities, parish and community councils are required to hold an annual meeting. The date for the annual meeting is fixed in accordance with provisions set out in the appropriate part of the Twelfth Schedule (see below).
(2) All parish meetings are required to assemble annually. There is no statutory requirement for community meetings to assemble annually.

Other meetings

In addition to the annual meeting, principal councils, joint authorities, parish councils and community councils may hold such other meetings as they may determine. However, parish councils must hold at least three other meetings in addition to the annual meeting.[1] Extraordinary meetings can be called by:

(a) the chairman at any time; or
(b) any five members of a principal council, or any three members of a joint authority, or any two members of a parish or community council, who requisition the chairman to call a meeting. If the chairman refuses or fails to call a meeting within seven days, a specified number of members may

---

1 Local Government Act 1972, Sch 12, Part II, para 8.

call the meeting themselves, the specified number being five for a principal council, three for a joint authority and two for a parish or community council. Those members who call the meeting are not required to be the same as those who make the requisition.[2]

In addition to the annual assembly of the parish and community meetings, parish meetings may hold such other meetings as the parish council or, if there is no parish council, the chairman of the parish meeting shall determine. A parish meeting which does not have a parish council is required to assemble at least twice a year. A community meeting may be convened at any time.

A parish meeting may be convened by the chairman of the parish council, or any two councillors for the parish, or any six local government electors for the parish. Where there is no parish council, a meeting may be convened by the chairman of the parish meeting or any person who represents the parish on the district council.[3]

A community meeting may be convened by the chairman of the community council, or any two councillors representing the community on the council, or by any six local government electors for the community.[4]

Places of meetings

Meetings of principal councils, joint authorities, parish and community councils may be held in such place as those bodies direct, either within or without the area of authority.

However, meetings of parish and community councils and parish and community meetings should not be held in premises licensed for the sale of intoxicating liquor unless no other suitable room is available either free of charge or at reasonable cost.[5]

Dates and times

(1) Times for annual meetings

The time for the annual meeting of councils is fixed by the council itself, or if no time is fixed, at 12 noon for principal councils and joint authorities and 6 pm for parish and community councils.

(2) Dates for annual meetings

(a) *Principal councils*
    (i) In an election year for councillors the annual meeting is to be held

---

2 Local Government Act 1972, Sch 12, Parts I, IA, II and IV, paras 3, 6B, 9 and 25.
3 Ibid, Sch 12, Part III, para 15(1).
4 Ibid, Sch 12, Part V, para 30(1).
5 Ibid, Sch 12, Parts II, III, IV and V, paras 10(1), 14(5), 26(1) and 32(2).

on the eighth day after the retirement of councillors or on a day within 21 days immediately following the day of retirement.

(ii) In a year where there is no election, the annual meeting is to be held on a day in March, April or May as the council may decide.

(b) Joint authorities

The annual meeting of a joint authority is to be held on a day in March, April or May as the authority may decide.

(c) Parish and community councils

(i) In an election year for councillors the annual meeting shall be held on or within 14 days after the day on which the councillors take office.

(ii) In a year where there is no election, the annual meeting shall take place on a day in May as the council may determine.

(d) Parish meetings

A parish meeting is to assemble annually on a day between 1 March and 1 June.

Summoning of meetings

(1) Principal councils, joint authorities, parish and community councils

Two steps must be taken to summon a meeting:

(a) Notice of the time and place of an intended meeting must be published at the offices of the body (or in the case of parish or community councils at some conspicuous place in the parish or the community) at least three clear days before the meeting. When the meeting is called by the members of the council, this notice must be signed by them and specify the proposed business.

(b) A summons to attend a meeting must be sent to every council member at least three clear days before the meeting. The summons must be signed by the proper officer of the council and specify the business proposed to be transacted at the meeting. If a summons is not served on every member of the council, the validity of the meeting is not affected. The day on which the notice is published or the summons sent and the day of the meeting are excluded for the purposes of calculating three clear days. There must be three whole days in between these two dates.[6] With one exception, no business shall be transacted at the meeting of a principal council unless it is specified in the summons. The exception enables urgent business to be

---

6 *R v Herefordshire Justices* (1820) 3 B & Ald 581.

brought before the meeting in accordance with the council's standing orders.[7]

(2) Parish and community councils

Public notice of the time and place of the intended meeting must be posted at some conspicuous place or places in the parish or the community. Public notice must also be given in any other manner in which the person convening the meeting considers desirable. The notice must be given at least seven clear days before the meeting. However, not less than 14 clear days' notice is required where the business proposed to be transacted at the meeting relates to either:

(a) the establishment or dissolution of a parish council; or
(b) the grouping of the parish with another parish or parishes under a common parish council or the grouping of the community with another community or communities under a common community council.

Chairman

(1) At the meetings of principal councils, joint authorities, parish councils and community councils the chairman presides. If the chairman is absent, the vice-chairman presides. In London borough councils, the deputy mayor, if chosen, presides in the absence of the mayor. If the chairman and vice-chairman are absent, and in the case of London borough councils the deputy mayor is either absent or is present but not chosen, the members of the council can chose another one of their members to preside.
(2) The chairman, or failing him or her, the vice-chairman of the parish council presides at parish meetings in the case of a parish having a parish council. In a parish without a parish council, the parish meeting is chaired by the chairman elected by the parish meeting at its annual assembly. The parish meeting may appoint a person to take the chair in the absence of the chairman and vice-chairman of the parish council, or the chairman of the parish meeting, as the case may be.
(3) The chairman of the community council presides at community meetings in the case of a community having a community council. In any other case, a community meeting appoints a person to be chairman of that meeting. Thus, there is no permanent chairman for such community meetings, unlike parish meetings.

---

7 Local Government Act 1972, Sch 12, Part I, para 4(5).

Quorum

A quorum must be present to empower a meeting to conduct business. The quorum is one-quarter of the members of the body for principal councils and joint authorities, and one-third for parish and community councils. The quorum must be a disinterested quorum, thus no member can be counted who is disabled from voting (see 'Disability to vote' below).

If more than one-third of the members of the body are disqualified, then the quorum is to be one-quarter of the remaining qualified members for a principal council and a joint authority, and one-third of the remaining qualified members for a parish and community council until the number of qualified members is increased to not less than two-thirds of the whole number of members of the authority. In no case can the quorum be less than three at a parish or community council.[8]

Voting

(1) The decisions of principal councils, joint authorities and parish and community councils are taken by the majority of the members present and voting at meetings. In the case of equality of votes the person presiding has the casting vote.[9] The prescribed method for voting at parish and community meetings is by a show of hands, unless the standing orders provide otherwise.[10] The names of members present at a meeting are required to be recorded. A member of a parish or community council may request that how each member voted on a particular question be recorded.

(2) The decisions of parish and community meetings are made by the majority of those present and voting. The person presiding at the meeting has the casting vote in the case of equality of votes. Unless a poll is demanded the decision of the person presiding as to the result of the voting is final. A poll may be demanded at any time before the conclusion of the meeting upon any matter arising during the meeting. For the demand to be effective, the person presiding must consent to the poll or it must be made by not less than 10, or one-third of the local government electors present, whichever is less.[11] A poll is taken of those entitled to attend the meeting and it is taken by ballot in accordance with rules made by statutory instrument.

---

8 Local Government Act 1972, Sch 12, Parts II and IV, paras 12 and 28.
9 Ibid, Sch 12, Part VI, para 39.
10 Ibid, Sch 12, Parts II and IV, paras 13 and 29.
11 Ibid, Sch 12, Parts III and V, paras 18 and 34.

Disability to vote

Any member of a principal council, joint authority, parish or community council who has any pecuniary interest, direct or indirect, in a contract or proposed contract or other matter and is present at a meeting at which it is to be considered must disclose his or her interest and must not discuss or vote upon that matter. Standing orders may provide for the exclusion of a member while a matter is being considered in which he or she is interested.[12]

A member having an indirect pecuniary interest in a contract, proposed contract or other matter by reason only of a beneficial interest in securities not exceeding £5,000 (or one-hundredth of the total nominal value of the issued share capital whichever is less) must declare his or her interest but is not prohibited from taking part in the discussion and voting.[13] An interest of a member which is so remote or insignificant that it cannot reasonably be regarded as likely to influence a member in discussing or voting on a matter is not treated as a pecuniary interest.[14]

General notice of an interest may be made to the proper officer of the authority. Such notice must be recorded in a book which is open to inspection by members of the council.[15]

Where disabilities would apply to so great a proportion of the council as to impede business, or in any other case where it is in the interests of the inhabitants of the area that the disabilities be removed, they may be removed by the direct council with respect to a member of a parish or community council, and by the Secretary of State with respect to a member of a principal council or joint authority.[16] The Secretary of State has removed the disability on council house tenants discussing and voting on matters of general housing policy.

Minutes

Minutes of the meetings of principal councils, joint authorities and parish and community councils must be entered into a book kept for that purpose. The book may consist of loose leaves consecutively numbered. The minutes must be signed by the person presiding at the meeting which they record, or at the next suitable meeting. Any minute purporting to be so signed is to be received in evidence without further proof.[17]

---

12 Local Government Act 1972, s 94.
13 Local Government and Housing Act 1989, Sch 11, para 23.
14 Local Government Act 1972, s 97(5).
15 Ibid, s 96.
16 Ibid, s 97.
17 Ibid, Sch 12, Part VI, para 41.

Similarly, minutes must be kept of the proceedings of parish and community meetings.[18]

Committees

Local authorities have a wide discretion to appoint committees to discharge their functions. By s 106 of the Local Government Act 1972, the quorum, proceedings and place of committees are determined by the committee itself, subject to standing orders made by the local authority.

Attendance by non-members

The Public Bodies (Admission to Meetings) Act 1960 provided that the meetings of principal councils, parish and community councils and parish meetings should normally be open to the public. Section 100 of the Local Government Act 1972 extended the provisions of the 1960 Act to committees, but not to sub-committees of local authorities. Thus, the potential existed for local authorities to avoid the right of the public to access by delegating the functions of committees to sub-committees. The Local Government (Access to Information) Act 1985 provides for greater public access to the meetings, reports and documents of principal councils, joint authorities and their committees and sub-committees.

Principal councils and joint authorities

(1) Access to meetings by the public and the press
The Local Government (Access to Information) Act 1985 amends s 100 of the Local Government Act 1972 by inserting a new Part VA (ss 100A–100K). Section 100A provides that the meetings of principal councils should normally be open to the public. The meetings of the committees and sub-committees of principal councils[19] and the meetings of joint authorities[20] and their committees and sub-committees should also be open to the public. However, there are certain circumstances in which the public can be denied access to the meetings of the above bodies.

The public *must* be excluded from a meeting where it is likely that confidential information would otherwise be disclosed in breach of an obligation of confidence.[21] Confidential information is information given to the council by a government department on terms which forbid the disclosure of information

---

18 Local Government Act, 1972, Sch 12, Parts III and V, paras 19 and 35.
19 By s 100E, the provisions of s 100A–D are applied to committees and sub-committees of principal councils as they apply to principal councils themselves.
20 By s 100J, joint authorities are included in any reference to a principal council in Part VA.
21 Local Government Act 1972, s 100A(2).

to the public and information the disclosure of which to the public is prohibited by or under any enactment or court order.[22]

The council *may* by resolution exclude the public from a meeting whenever it is likely that exempt information would otherwise be disclosed.[23] Thus, there is no duty to exclude the public, merely a discretion to do so. If there is a resolution to exclude members of the public from a meeting, it must identify the proceedings or part of the proceedings to which it applies and state the category of exempt information which the exclusion is based upon in terms of the descriptions of exempt information in Sch 12A.[24]

Schedule 12A categorises the following information as exempt:

(a) information relating to employees or officers of the authority (past, present or applicants to become);

(b) information relating to occupiers (past or present) of accommodation provided by or at the expense of the authority, and information relating to an applicant to become an occupier;

(c) information relating to applicants for, or recipients (past or present) of services or financial assistance provided by or at the expense of the authority;

(d) information relating to the adoption, care, fostering or education of any particular child;

(e) information relating to the financial or business affairs of any particular person;

(f) the amount of proposed expenditure by the authority for the acquisition of property or the supply of goods or services, if and so long as disclosure would give an advantage to a person entering into or seeking to enter into a contract with the authority with respect of property, goods or services;

(g) any terms proposed or to be proposed by or to the authority in negotiations for a contract for the acquisition of property or the supply of goods or services, if and so long as disclosure to the public would prejudice the authority in those or any other negotiations for such a contract;

(h) the identity of an authority or person as the person offering a tender for a contract for the supply of goods or services;

(i) information relating to consultations or negotiations (actual or contemplated) concerning a labour relations matter, if and so long as disclosure would prejudice the authority in those or other negotiations or consultations of such a nature;

(j) information relating to legal advice or legal proceedings;

(k) information which would reveal that the authority proposes to serve a notice, or make an order or direction under any enactment if and so

---

22 Local Government Act 1972, s 100A(3).

23 Ibid, s 100A(4).

24 Ibid, s 100A(5).

long as disclosure might provide the person to be affected with an opportunity to defeat the purpose of the notice, order or direction;

(l) any action to be taken in connection with the prevention, investigation or prosecution of crime; and

(m) the identity of a protected informant.

At least three clear days' public notice of the time and place of a meeting must be given at the offices of the body. If the meeting is convened at shorter notice than three days, public notice of the time and place of the meeting must be given at the time it is convened. While the meeting is open to the public the council does not have a power to exclude members of the public from the meeting. Duly accredited press representatives are, so far as reasonably practicable, to be afforded facilities for taking their report and for telephoning it at their own expense.[25] However, the above provisions do not affect the common law power to exclude the public and the press to suppress or prevent disorderly conduct or other misbehaviour at a meeting.[26]

(2) Access to agendas and reports

Copies of the agenda and any report for the meeting must be open to public inspection at the offices of the body at least three clear days before the meeting, or when the meeting is convened at shorter notice, copies must be available from the time the meeting is convened. Items which are added to the agenda and reports relating to those items must be open to public inspection from the time they are added. However, copies of the agenda or report are not required to be open to public inspection until copies are available to members of the council.[27]

An item of business cannot be considered at a meeting unless a copy of the agenda including that item has been open to public inspection for the required length of time, or by reason of special circumstances, which shall be specified in the minutes, the chairman of the meeting is of the opinion that the item should be considered as a matter of urgency.[28]

If the proper officer is of the opinion that during the consideration of certain items the meeting is unlikely to be open to the public, part or whole of a report which relates to those items may be withheld from public inspection.[29] Where part or whole of a report is withheld, the proper officer must mark every copy of the report, or part of it, 'not for publication' and state under which category of exempt information the public are likely to be excluded by the council when it considers the item to which the report relates.[30]

Where a meeting or part of it is required to be open to the public, a reasonable number of copies of the agenda and reports for the meeting must

---

25 Local Government Act 1972, s 100A(6).
26 Ibid, s 100A(8).
27 Ibid, s 100B(1) and (3).
28 Ibid, s 100B(4).
29 Ibid, s 100B(2).
30 Ibid, s 100B(5).

be made available for the use of members of the public present at the meeting.[31] The press shall, on request and on payment of postage and other necessary charge for transmission, be supplied with a copy of the agenda and reports for the meeting, such further statements as are necessary to indicate the nature of the items included in the agenda and, if the proper officer thinks fit in the case of any item, copies of any other documents supplied to members of the council in connection with the item.[32]

If the proper officer is of the opinion that during the consideration of certain items the meeting is unlikely to be open to the public, part or whole of a report which relates to those items may be withheld from copies of reports supplied to the public at a meeting, and supplied to the press on request.[33]

(3) Access to minutes

The minutes or copy of the minutes of a meeting must be open to public inspection for six years after the meeting at the offices of the body.[34] Minutes disclosing exempt information during the consideration of which the public were excluded from the meeting are excluded from the requirement to be open for public inspection. However, where such an exclusion results in the minutes available not providing the public with a reasonably fair and coherent record of whole or part of the proceedings the proper officer must make a written summary of the proceedings, or the part, which provides a reasonably fair and coherent record without disclosing the exempt information.[35] Such a summary must be open to public inspection for six years.

A copy of the agenda of the meeting and a copy of any report for the meeting relating to items during which the meeting was open to the public shall be open to public inspection for six years after the meeting at the offices of the body.

(4) Access to background papers

Background papers are those documents which disclose any facts or matters on which in the opinion of the proper officer the report or an important part of it is based and which have in his or her opinion been relied on to a material extent in preparing the report. They do not include any published works.[36] If, and so long as, copies of the whole or part of a report for a meeting are required to be open to public inspection, copies of a list of background papers for the report or part of the report and at least one copy of each of the documents included in that list must also be open to public inspection.[37] The list of background papers and the papers themselves (if appropriate) need only be available for public inspection for four years.[38] The list need not include any

---

31 Local Government Act 1972, s 100B(6).
32 Ibid, s 100B(7).
33 Ibid, s 100B(8).
34 Ibid, s 100C(1).
35 Ibid, s 100C(2).
36 Ibid, s 100D(5).
37 Ibid, s 100D(1).
38 Ibid, s 100D(2).

document which discloses exempt information, nor any document which, if open to public inspection, would disclose confidential information.[39]

(5) Supplemental provisions

A document which is required to be open to inspection shall be so open at all reasonable hours. Except in the case of background papers (where a reasonable fee is payable), no payment may be required for the facility.[40] A person may make copies of or extracts from a document required to be open to inspection, or may require a photocopy to be made upon payment of an appropriate fee.[41] Where accessible documents are open to public inspection, or are supplied to the public or press, the publication of defamatory matter in such documents is privileged unless published with malice.[42]

Parish and community councils and parish meetings

The Public Bodies (Admission to Meetings) Act 1960 continues to govern the access of the public and press to meetings of parish and community councils and parish meetings. The Act provides that the meetings of such bodies should normally be open to the public. However, by s 1(2) of the Public Bodies (Admission to Meetings) Act 1960, a body may, by resolution, exclude the public from a meeting whenever publicity would be prejudicial to the public interest by reason of the confidential nature of the business to be transacted or for other 'special reasons' stated in the resolution and arising from the nature of the business or proceedings. Receiving advice or recommendations from an outside person, not a member, committee or sub-committee of the body, is a special reason why publicity would be prejudicial to the public interest.[43] Receiving advice from officers has been held to amount to a special reason.[44] The requirement to record special reasons in a resolution has been held to be directory not mandatory. Therefore, the fact that special reasons are not adequately recorded does not invalidate the resolution of a body to exclude the public.[45]

Where a meeting is required to be open to the public, three clear days' public notice of the time and place of the meeting must be given by posting it at the offices of the body (or, if the body has no offices, in some conspicuous place in the area). If the meeting is called at shorter notice than three days then public notice must be given at the time it is convened.[46]

39 Local Government Act 1972, s 100D(4).
40 Ibid, s 100H(1).
41 Ibid, s 100H(2).
42 Ibid, s 100H(5).
43 Public Bodies (Admission to Meetings) Act 1960, s 1(3).
44 *R v Liverpool City Council ex parte Liverpool Taxi Fleet Operators' Association* [1975] 1 WLR 701.
45 Ibid.
46 Public Bodies (Admission to Meetings) Act 1960, s 1(4)(a).

The press shall, on request and payment of postage and other necessary charge for transmission, be supplied with a copy of the agenda, such further statements and particulars as are necessary to indicate the nature of the items included in the agenda and, if thought fit in the case of any item, copies of any other reports or documents supplied to members of the council in connection with the item.[47] Publication of defamatory matter contained in the agenda or other information supplied is privileged unless published with malice.[48]

While the meeting is open to the public, the body shall not have the power to exclude members of the public from the meeting and duly accredited press representatives are so far as reasonably practicable to be given facilities for taking their report and for telephoning it at their own expense.[49] The above provisions do not affect the common law power of exclusion to suppress or prevent disorderly conduct or other misbehaviour at a meeting.[50]

The minutes of a meeting of a parish or community council or parish meeting are open to inspection by local government electors for the area. They may also be inspected by an agent of a local government elector.[51]

---

47 Public Bodies (Admission to Meetings) Act 1960, s 1(4)(b).
48 Ibid, s 1(5).
49 Ibid, s 1(4)(c).
50 Public Bodies (Admission to Meetings) Act 1960, s 1(8). See also *R v Brent Health Authority, ex parte Francis* [1985] QB 869, in which it was held that s 1(8) preserves the common law power in the chairman to exclude the public if it is clear that their intention is to disrupt the transaction of business at the meeting. (Local Government Act 1972, s 100A(8) is virtually identical to s 1(8) of the 1960 Act.)
51 Local Government Act 1972, s 228 (as amended by the Local Government (Access to Information) Act 1985).

APPENDIX

PRECEDENTS FOR COMPANY MEETINGS

CONTENTS

These precedents are based on selected precedents from *Secretarial Administration* (Jordans, 1994).

1 Notice of board meeting

(On the company's notepaper)

Notice is hereby given that a meeting of the directors will be held at [*place*] on [*date*] at [*time*] at which your presence is requested.
....
Secretary

[*Date of notice*]

Editor's Note
In suitable circumstances the agenda for the meeting may be set out below.

2   Specimen agenda for board meeting

AGENDA

1. Minutes of meeting held on ....
2. Report from managing director.
3. Management accounts at [*date*].
4. Special matters:

[*List*]

5. Transfers of shares.
6. Sealings since last meeting.

3 Annual general meeting

(a) Notice and agenda

NOTICE IS HEREBY GIVEN that the annual general meeting of the company will be held at [*place*] on [*date*] at [*time*] for the following purposes:

1. To receive the report of the directors and the audited accounts for the year ended ...... 19... (and to declare a dividend).
2. To elect the directors in place of those retiring (see the directors' report).
3. To re-elect the auditors.
4. To authorise the directors to fix the remuneration of the auditors.
5. To transact any other ordinary business of the company.

By order of the board

....

Secretary

[*Registered office address*]

Dated ...... 19...

A member entitled to attend and vote at this meeting is entitled to appoint one or more proxies to attend and vote in his or her stead. A proxy need not be a member of the company.

NOTE – Copies of service contracts of the directors with the company and any subsidiaries not expiring or determinable without payment of compensation within one year will be available for inspection at the registered office during normal business hours until the conclusion of the meeting.

(b) Specimen minutes

Minutes of the (10th) annual general meeting held at [*place*] on [*date*].

Present: .... (Chairman)
.... (Director)
.... (Director)
.... (Director)
.... (Director)

(and the members who signed the attendance sheet attached to these minutes).

In attendance:

> .... (Secretary)
> .... (Auditors)
> (and ....
> ....)

1. The secretary read the notice of meeting.

2. Ms .... on behalf of the auditors read the report of the auditors.

3. The chairman proposed:

   'That the report of the directors and the audited accounts for the year ended ...... 19..., now submitted to this meeting, be and are hereby received and:

   *That the final dividend of ...p per share recommended therein be and is hereby declared payable on ...... 19... to holders of ordinary shares registered at the close of business on ...... 19...,'

   *'That no dividend be paid.'

   Mr .... seconded the resolution, which was put to the meeting and declared carried.

4. The chairman proposed:

   'That ....
   the director(s) retiring by rotation be and is (are) hereby re-elected (a) director(s) of the company.'

   Mrs .... seconded the resolution, which was put to the meeting and declared carried.

5. The chairman proposed:

   'That the appointment(s) of .... to the board on ...... 19... be confirmed.'

Editor's Note
Under Table A any director appointed since the previous annual general meeting retires at the annual general meeting.

   Mr .... seconded the resolution, which was put to the meeting and declared carried.

6. The chairman proposed:

   'That Messrs .... be and are hereby re-elected as auditors of the company, to hold office until the conclusion of the next annual general meeting.'

   Mr .... seconded the resolution, which was put to the meeting and declared carried.

7. Mrs ...., a member, proposed:

'That the remuneration of Messrs ...., the company auditors, be fixed by the directors in respect of the period ending at the conclusion of the next annual general meeting.'

Ms ...., another member, seconded the resolution, which was put to the meeting and declared carried.

8. There being no further business the meeting was closed.

....
Chairman

————————————

*Delete as appropriate.

4   Extraordinary general meeting: form of notice to propose extraordinary or special resolution

Notice is hereby given that an extraordinary general meeting of the company will be held at [*place*] on [*date*] at [*time*] when the following resolution will be proposed as an (*extraordinary) (*special) resolution:

[*Resolution*]

By order of the board
....
Secretary

[*Registered office address*]
Dated .... 19......

----

*Delete as appropriate

Editor's Note
For note as to proxies at an annual general meeting, see **3(a) Notice and agenda** above.

5 Special notice

(a) Form of special notice

The Directors   [*Date*]
.... PLC

I hereby give special notice of my intention to propose at the annual general meeting of the company to be convened for ...... 19... that Mr ...... be re-elected a director of the company notwithstanding that he has attained the age of 70.

I am the registered holder of ... ordinary shares in the capital of the company.

Yours faithfully
....

(b) Special notice resolution in agenda for annual general meeting

Extract from notice of annual general meeting:

To re-elect directors:

1. Mrs .... who has attained the age of 70. (Special notice to propose this resolution has been received.)

6   Agreement to short notice for an extraordinary general meeting

(a) *To consider ordinary resolutions*

FORM OF CONSENT: ORDINARY RESOLUTIONS

To the directors of .... Limited

We, the undersigned, being the holders of 95 per cent in nominal value of the shares of the above-named company do hereby testify our consent to an extraordinary general meeting of the above-named company being held on the ...... day of ...... 19... (notwithstanding that the meeting is called by shorter notice than that specified in s 369 of the Companies Act 1985), for the purpose of considering the ordinary resolutions set out in the notice convening the said meeting, a copy whereof has, for the purpose of identification, been signed by us.

(b) *To consider special resolutions*

FORM OF CONSENT: SPECIAL RESOLUTIONS

To the directors of .... Limited

We, the undersigned, being the holders of 95 per cent in nominal value of the shares of the above-named company do hereby testify our consent to an extraordinary general meeting of the above-named company being held on the ...... day of ...... 19... (notwithstanding that the meeting is called by shorter notice than that specified in s 378 of the Companies Act 1985), for the purpose of considering the special resolutions set out in the notice convening the said meeting, a copy whereof has, for the purpose of identification, been signed by us.

(c) *To consider ordinary and special resolutions*

FORM OF CONSENT: ORDINARY AND SPECIAL RESOLUTIONS

To the directors of .... Limited

We, the undersigned, being the holders of 95 per cent in nominal value of the shares of the above-named company do hereby testify our consent to an extraordinary general meeting of the above-named company being held on the

...... day of ...... 19... (notwithstanding that the meeting is called by shorter notice than that specified in ss 369 and 378 of the Companies Act 1985), for the purpose of considering the ordinary and special resolutions set out in the notice convening the said meeting, a copy whereof has, for the purpose of identification, been signed by us.

Editor's Notes
1. A notice of the meeting prepared in the usual form must be delivered to the respective members before this waiver is signed.
2. These precedents assume that an elective resolution to reduce the requisite majority from 95 per cent to 90 per cent is not in force. If such an elective resolution is in force, amend the percentage specified accordingly.

7   Agreement to short notice for an annual general meeting

FORM OF CONSENT: ANNUAL GENERAL MEETING

To the directors of .... Limited

We, the undersigned, being all the members entitled to attend and vote at general meetings of the above-named company do hereby testify our consent to the annual general meeting of the above-named company being held on the ...... day of ...... 19... (notwithstanding that the meeting is called by shorter notice than that specified in s 369 of the Companies Act 1985) [and do hereby agree that copies of the documents required to be sent in accordance with s 238 of the Companies Act 1985 shall be deemed to have been duly sent notwithstanding that they are sent less than 21 days before the date of the said meeting].

Editor's Note

If an elective resolution is in force to dispense with the requirement that accounts and reports be laid before the company in general meeting, the words in brackets will not be required.

8 Written resolution of members in lieu of meeting pursuant to Companies Act 1985, s 381A

COMPANY NUMBER

THE COMPANIES ACTS 1985 TO 1989

PRIVATE COMPANY LIMITED BY SHARES

WRITTEN RESOLUTION(S) OF

.... LIMITED

Dated this .... day of .... 19...

WRITTEN RESOLUTION(S)

We, the undersigned, being all the members of the company who, at the date of this resolution would be entitled to attend and vote at general meetings of the company HEREBY PASS the following resolutions as [an] [ ]* resolution(s) [**] and agree that the said resolution(s) shall for all purposes be as valid and effective as if the same had been passed by us all at a general meeting of the company duly convened and held:

*Elective
 Special
 Extraordinary
 Ordinary

**if a class resolution, details here:
    ie 'of the class of seven per cent cumulative preference shares in the capital of the'

9 Form of proxy

ANNUAL GENERAL MEETING

I, the undersigned, being a member of the above-named company, hereby appoint Mrs ...., or failing her Mr .... or the chairman of the meeting, as my proxy to vote for me on my behalf at the (fifty-sixth) annual general meeting of the company, notice of which was sent to the shareholders with the directors' report and accounts for the year 19..., and at any adjournment thereof. The proxy will vote on the under-mentioned resolutions, as indicated:

Resolutions	For	Against
1. To receive the directors' report and accounts for the year ended ...... and to confirm dividends.	☐	☐
2. To re-elect ...... as a director.	☐	☐
3. To re-appoint the retiring auditors, and to authorise the directors to fix the remuneration of the auditors.	☐	☐
4. The resolution (item 4 in the notice of the above-mentioned meeting) relating to the allotment of securities.	☐	☐
5. The resolution (item 5 in the notice) relating to the amendment of clause ... of the company's articles of association.	☐	☐

If this form is signed and returned without any indication as to how the proxy shall vote, he or she will exercise his discretion both as to how to vote (and whether or not to abstain from voting).

Signed ...... 19...

Signature: ....

NOTE – To be valid, this form of proxy must be deposited at the registered office of the company not less than 48 hours before the time for holding the meeting.

Editor's Note
Deposit of proxy form 48 hours before meeting reflects Table A, reg 62.

10 Elective resolutions

(a) Section 366A – election to dispense with annual general meeting

'ELECTIVE RESOLUTION'

'That pursuant to Section 366A of the Companies Act 1985 the Company hereby elects to dispense with the holding of Annual General Meetings in 19... and subsequent years until this election is revoked.'

Editor's Note: This election has effect in the year in which it is made and subsequent years, but does not affect any liability already incurred by reason of default in holding an annual general meeting.

(b) Section 252 – election to dispense with laying of accounts and reports before general meeting

'ELECTIVE RESOLUTION'

'That pursuant to Section 252 of the Companies Act 1985 the Company hereby elects to dispense with the laying of accounts and reports before the Company in General Meeting' [for the current financial year and all subsequent financial years].

Editor's Note
This election has effect in relation to the accounts and reports in respect of the financial year in which it is passed, and subsequent financial years, but *not* previous financial years.

INDEX